This cookbook came about as a desire to preserve the memory of a beautiful bond between eight women. As it progressed, it became a reclaiming of the feminine and the domestic arts among women. As a graduate student (again), I have been exposed to much rhetoric and research concerning feminism. While I appreciate the efforts of many women who have blazed the trail in feminine freedom, I have striven to find my place on this continuum of study.

I have learned that women of America have gone through many waves of feminism, from suffrage, to economizing and capitalizing domesticity (home economics), to establishing careers, to bra burning. I have respectfully read and listened to these varying views. I have also, however, become increasingly aware of the 21st century revival of the domestic arts. They have cycled through the waves of feminism and made their ways back to girls and women across America. I see it in popular television channels, magazines, and websites. With the rise of FOOD Network, HGTV, Pinterest, and Etsy, girls in particular are reclaiming for themselves those domestic arts that were abandoned by others of their gender just decades before. So what is the difference now? My conclusion would be one word: choice.

In the beginning of this cookbook project, I asked Grammie if she ever felt like she had no other choice but to marry and have children. Her answer was a firm "no," said in an aggravated tone. She and her six sisters were given every opportunity to be whoever they wanted to be, and yet, each girl chose a life of homemaking and motherhood. Some of the sisters chose to work outside the home but never at the cost of their families. They haven't lived according to anyone's expectations, rather, their own desires. The familial nurture that they received influenced their desire to nurture. Consequently, they are menders, quietly knitting holes in the world with their love. They are individual women who have had independent thoughts, feelings, and goals, and all of those attributes included their most sacred of their relationships: their families.

I have painted an image for each sister. These effigies are to honor the memories of each of these strands of Pearl. They are illustrations of the simplest kind: an ice cream freezer, a rose, an electric mixer, a pie etc. And yet, in the midst of their simplicity is a deep, rich sentimentality that grips each generation that has followed these beautiful women. The threads of their lives have been woven in their descendants and because of them, I am a proud domestic artist!

This book is dedicated to my Grammie, Tommie Jean Melton Akin. She has taught me what it means to be a lady. I love you Grammie.

- Mandy

Details about the paintings:

Burial is a large southern tradition. I enjoy a nice ride into the country where I travel to cemeteries here in the south, taking sheets of vellum and conte crayons. Through light research, I have learned that much of the cemetery art is quite meaningful and that the symbolism on many of the head stones is quite subversive. I also love the look of the low relief transferred in black conte which gives the impression of wrought iron and looks vaguely like the brass rubbings of old Europe. After rubbing the impression from a headstone, I typically lay a rock on the epitaph (following a Jewish tradition) and say a prayer for the family of the one who has passed. This entire process is so deep and inspiring to me, seeing the mortality of life before my eyes and yet pondering the legacy that these people left to the world in which I live. I am especially drawn to the graves of women: sisters, mothers, daughters. They are adventuresses, teachers, lovers, friends, and care-givers, all usually marked by their relationships and care that they gave to others. I tried to find grave rubbings which were indicative of how each sister's legacy has touched me.

I apply these vellum rubbings to my panels using clear acrylic gloss medium, as it makes the vellum transparent and the rubbing shows as almost a ghostlike image. It is as though the memory of those who have passed still leave their marks and I feel as if I am in some small way paying tribute to them.

The biology of the pearl is a complex and interesting one: as a piece of sand intrudes upon the muscle inside an oyster shell, it begins to irritate the living organism. As a means of protection, the oyster secretes the nacre, or mother- of- pearl, from the shell onto the irritant, creating a protective coating.

My use of the pearls and pearlescent paint is not only a reference to Big Mama's name but also to her nurturing and "forming" her "pearls" or girls. In turn, the girls have passed down their legacies and domestic arts to their successors, creating strands of pearls. But the number three in the use of the strands suggest the Holy Trinity and a deeper spiritual legacy that Big Mama and her daughters have passed down to their children, grandchildren, great grandchildren, and so on.

I like the amber shellac because of its "honey" appearance, an artistic reference to the biological sisterhood of honeybees. I also find pleasure in the gloss and age effect that it gives the surface. I chose to age parts and make some remain bright, both for the same reason: these ladies' legacies will live (liveliness of the paint) but they will do so far beyond their lifetimes (age of the shellac). They are "golden," ageless spirits in the face of time. In addition to the honeybee suggestion, I also used handmade stamped paper which bears the image of an elephant, a symbol for matriarchy and sisterhood.

Melvin Cooper (left), Martha Cooper (right),
Luna (middle), Pearl (baby), Oscar (left front),
and Birdwell (right front)

Pearl (left) and Louise (right) Coop

Pearl Jeanette Cooper was born August
18, 1899. She was the fourth of seven
children to Melvin and Martha Smith
Cooper.

Hubert Sample Melton was also born
in February 25, 1899. He was the first
of four children to Jesse T. Melton and
Gennie Sample Melton.

Hubert Sample Melton

Pearl (Big Mama) and Sample (Big Daddy) grew up in the same Grandview community in Rusk county, Texas. Their farms were near one another and as children, they played together. They were lifelong friends and companions.

Sample and Pearl married in 1919. From 1920 to 1935, they gave birth to seven daughters: Frances Elizabeth (Auntie), Dorothy Rae (Dot), Nila June (June), Betty Sue, Anna Kathryn (Kat), Patricia Ann (Patsy), and Tommie Jean.

When Sample was in his twenties, he and a hired hand were working in the fields when a storm came. They rushed for shelter beneath a tree; however, lightning struck the tree, killing the hired hand who was leaning against it and throwing Sample into nearby water, causing him to suffer severe shock. His physical health suffered and was ever the same after the incident. He battled a life of illness; however, he worked hard and provided for his family.

The Cooper Family

STANDING - RIGHT TO LEFT   SUMMER OF 1918   IN FRONT OF OLD COOPER HOME
                                    @ GRANDVIEW (OUTSIDE HENDERSON, TEXAS)

BIRDWELL COOPER, FAYE (STANDARD) COOPER, LUNA (COOPER) DORSEY,

VERNON COOPER, OSCAR COOPER, MARY (MELTON) COOPER,

SAMPLE MELTON, PEARL (COOPER) MELTON, JACK COOPER

SEATED - LEFT TO RIGHT

.   SMITH, MATTIE OR MARTHA COOPER, MARIE COOPER (BABY)

LOUISE (COOPER) DORSEY, MELVIN COOPER

note: the names of those in standing order are actually left to right.

A Cooper Family Reunion

BACK ROW - RIGHT TO LEFT

FRONT OF VERNON

ENNETTE (MELTON) COOPER, LOWELL COOPER (CHILD), VERNON COOPER (HOLDIN CHILD) DONALD COOPER,

MARY (MELTON) COOPER, MILDRID (COOPER) DORSEY, ALFUS DORSEY, OSCAR COOPER (TALL MAN BACK ROW)

ATHRYN (MELTON) RICHARDSON (FROUND ON FACE) LOUISE (COOPER) DORSEY, BURRIS DORSEY (BALD)

UNA (COOPER) DORSEY (FAT IN CENTER), CALVIN BARBER (TALL BACK ROW), MARIE (COOPER) BARBER,

UNE (MELTON) STOKLEY, TALMAGE COOPER (KILLED IN WW II) PEARL (COOPER) MELTON,

DOROTHY (MELTON) AKIN, CLETAS COOPER (BACK ROW), MILFORD DORSEY, KENNETH DORSEY,

ACK COOPER, FAYE (STANDARD) COOPER, MODINE (BROWN) COOPER, BIRDWELL COOPER
(END OF ROW)

FRONT ROW - LEFT TO RIGHT

OMMIE (MELTON) AKIN, CAROLYN (COOPER) CARTWRIGHT, RICHARD COOPER, KENNETH DORSEY

PATSY (MELTON) WALKER LEE, MELVIN COOPER, MELVIN COOPER, MARTHA (SMITH) COOPER,

OREN DORSEY, DALE COOPER, MARIDTH COOPER, BETTY (MELTON) JARRELL

Aunt Louise's Pineapple Cake

Aunt Louise's Pineapple Cake

2 cups sugar
⅔ cup Crisco
2¼ cups flour
2 eggs
1 cup milk
1 teaspoon vanilla
2½ teaspoons baking powder
pinch of salt

Icing
small can pineapple
2 cups sugar
½ cup water
3 tablespoon flour
½ stick butter
cook until thick

pineapple
flavoring
½ banana
juice

Beat shortening and sugar. Add eggs and vanilla and mix well. Sift together dry ingredients. Add milk and dry ingredients. To shortening, sugar, and egg mixture, alternating between milk and dry, ending with dry. Pour into (2) 9" pans or a 9"x13" cake pan. Bake at 350 degrees approximately 20-25 minutes (or until toothpick or cake tester comes out clean when inserted into the center).

Aunt Louise's Pie Crust
(Donna's handwriting)

Pie Crust	by Betty
1 stick butter - melted	2 T powered sugar
1 cup flour - heaping	1¼ C pecans - press in bottom of crust

Pie Crust	
1 c flour	1½ t salt
5 T Crisco - heaping	2½ T ice water

Louise Cooper Dorsey

Big Mama's baby sister and closest friend, was Louise Cooper Dorsey. (Aunt) Louise inherited the Cooper house, which is still in the family today.

Every Sunday Morning, Louise travelled the 6 miles into Henderson to sing on the Sunday morning radio program at local station KGRI. Afterwards, she drove back out to Grandview to attend her church.

ooper Home in Grandview, 1915 (built in 1912)

Today, the Cooper house is owned by David Dorsey, grandson of Louise Cooper Dorsey. With the house came 120 acres. He and his wife, Donna, have striven to keep the history of the home and originality of its structure.

ABOUT 1915
COOPER FAMILY GROUP - OLD HOME AT GRANDVIEW - HENDERSON, TEX

PEARL COOPER MELTON - FRONT ON LEFT
LOUISE COOPER DORSEY - 2ND
OPEL COOPER   - 3RD (DIED FEB 1913) 7 YRS OLD OF MEASLES
MATTIE COOPER - MAMA - 4TH
MELVIN COOPER - PAPA - 5TH
LUNA COOPER DORSEY - 6TH
DEWEY SMITH   - 7TH   NEPHEW OF MATTIE SMITH COOPER
OSCAR COOPER   - 8TH
JACK COOPER   - BACK ON LEFT
VERNON COOPER   - 2ND

Cooper Home in Grandview, 2012

Grandview Church Children

The lady in the hat is Gennie Sample Melton, wife of Jesse T. Melton and Mother of Hubert Sample Melton.

Grandmother Melton was the Sunday school teacher at the Grandview Baptist Church. Tommie says that she was also an excellent seamstress and created many of hers and Patsy's dresses made from her own homemade patterns.

After Sample and Pearl married, they left Grandview community and moved to the Jacobs community, just north of Grandview and then Joinerville where the East Texas oil boom occured.

When Tommie was 2 months old, moved and settled in Minden where Sample established a small dairy farm.

Old Minden Church

Where the Melton girls (who were still home), attended church. Tommie was baptized here. Although the old church has been destroyed, another building has been erected and Minden Church still remains.

July 1954

Left to right: Frances, Dorothy, June, Betty, Kathryn, Patsy, and Tommie

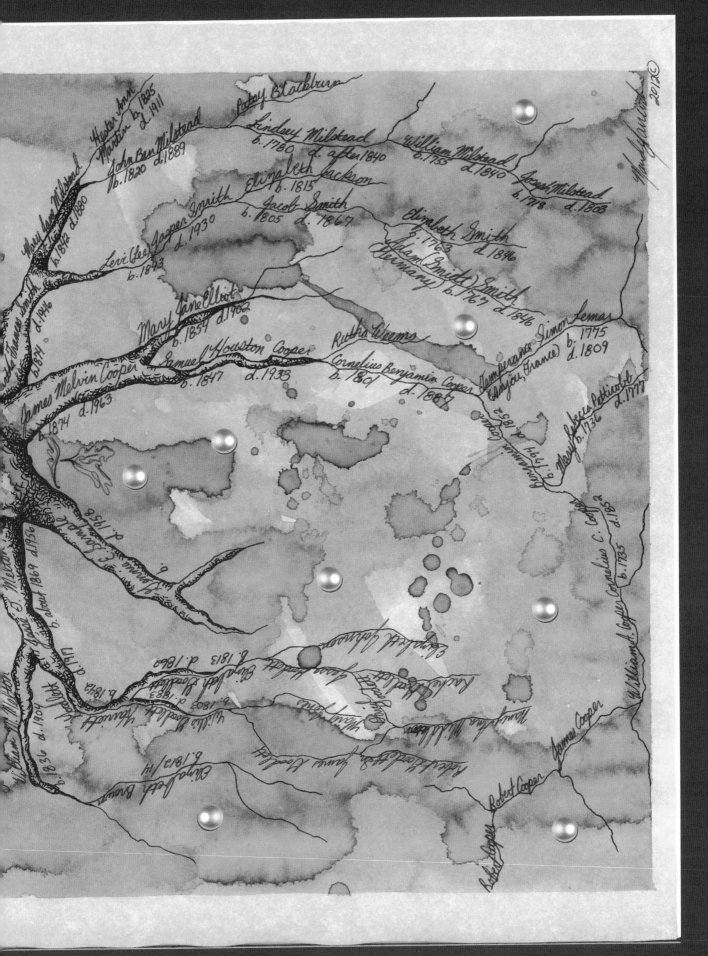

Pearl Jeanette
Cooper Melton

Photo by Rebecca Haskell

Born: August 1, 1899
Married: Hubert Sample Melton
Children: Frances, Dorothy, June,
Betty, Kathryn, Patsy, and Tommie
Died: 1987

Mother Pearl
20"x35"
Acrylic paint, gold leaf, grave rubbing, and faux pearls on wooden
panel

Tucked away in plastic bins in my storage room are a collection of
Blue Willow plates. Some are chipped and many are missing from the
collection. Certain pieces are even displayed throughout my house.
But because space does not allow all the pieces to be showcased, for
now they must remain safe, wrapped in brown paper and carefully
packed away.

Most of these beautiful pieces are brown where there was previously
ceramic glaze and all of the glazing is crazed with cracks of tender
usage. This precious china (marked "Japan") belonged to Mother Pearl,
Big Mama.

I remember being a toddler and sitting at the bar at her house on
Pine Street in Henderson, eating new potatoes in a white cream sauce
(a recipe that was indicative of Big Mama's culinary expertise and
uniqueness). She served me this delectable meal of potatoes and cream
on a Blue Willow saucer. I am convinced that the saucer itself added to
the experience of the meal and is part of the reason I love new potatoes
and cream sauce to this very day.

I also remember being a toddler and eating with my cousins at a small
table which was set up in the middle of the same kitchen in the same
house on the same street in the same town as mentioned in my
previously recorded potato memory. I recall my mother fixing me
a small plate of a fried chicken leg. Knowing my mother, I am sure
there were vegetables on that plate as well, but in my memory, I can
only recollect a chicken leg (from which I only ate all of the crust) and
a Blue Willow saucer. It was the best fried chicken crust I ever ate…
because it was served on Big Mama's Blue Willow, of course.

Big Mama's Amber Pie
(makes (2) 9" pies)

6 egg yolks
2 1/2 c. sugar
1 Tbsp. butter (melted)
2 Tbsp. flour
1 tsp. cinnamon
1 tsp. allspice
3 Tbsp. vinegar
1 c. raisins
1 c. buttermilk

Mix flour, sugar, and spices. Beat egg yolks and add sugar mixture, butter, raisins, vinegar, and buttermilk. Bake in unbaked pie shell at 325 degrees for 45 minutes. Top with meringue (see banana pudding) and brown.

Big Mama's Banana Pudding

1 ½ c. sugar
3 Tbsp.s of flour
3 eggs
3 c. milk (1 tall can evaporated milk and finish with whole milk)
1 tsp. vanilla
2 Tbsp.s butter

Mix flour and sugar. Beat egg yolks and add milk. Pour the egg and milk into the flour/ sugar mixture. Pour into a 2 qt. saucepan and bring to a boil, stirring constantly. Once it comes to a boil, turn burner down to medium heat but continue stirring until the mixture thickens. Take off the burner and add butter and vanilla.

Layer vanilla wafers on bottom of a 2 ½ qt. dish, followed by a layer of bananas on top. Pour the pudding on top of the cookies and bananas.

In a separate bowl, beat the egg whites along with ¼ tsp. of cream of tartar until foamy. Add 6 Tbsp.s of sugar, one at a time (always 2 per egg white) and beat until stiff and add 1 tsp. vanilla. Spread atop the pudding and bake at 325degrees until brown.

Big Mama's Applesauce Cake
(her handwriting)

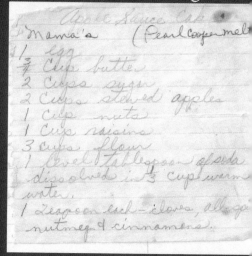

Apple Sauce Cake
Mama's   (Pearl Cooper melt
1 egg
¾ Cup butter
2 cups sugar
2 cups stewed apples
1 cup nuts
1 cup raisins
3 cups flour
1 level tablespoon of soda
dissolved in ⅓ cup warm water.
1 teaspoon each – cloves, allspice
nutmeg & cinnamon.

Applesauce Cake
(Big Mama's)
1 egg
¾ cup butter
2 cups sugar
2 cups stewed apples or applesauce
1 cup nuts   # ½ t. salt
1 cup raisins
3 cups flour
1 level tablespoon soda, dissolved
in ⅓ cup warm water
1 t. each cloves, allspice
nutmeg & cinnamon
Melt or soften butter, put
in sugar & egg, mix well.
Next add soda & apples. Add
nuts or raisins. Add flour
mixture slowly. Use tube
pan. Cook about 1½ hrs. ck with toothpick
350 degrees

Big Mama's Butternut Pie
(Tommie's Handwriting)

1 1/2 c. sugar
2 c. milk
1/2 c. flour
2 eggs
2 Tbsp. browned butter
1 tsp. vanilla

In a cast iron skillet, brown the butter. In a separate bowl, combine all other ingredients EXCEPT vanilla. After the butter has browned (careful not to burn), whisk in the combined mixture, stirring until very thick. When done, stir in vanilla and pour into a baked pie shell. Add meringue (see banana pudding) and brown.

Big Mama's Chicken and Dumplings

(1.) 3 lb. chicken (whole dressed)
Cover chicken in stock pot w/ about 6 C. Water. Add 2 tsp. salt, One small onion quartered, 1 stick celery or celery powder (1 tsp) 1 clove garlic or 1 tsp. garlic powder, and 1 whole carrot. Bring to boil on Med. Heat and cook until meat pulls from bone (temp. 160°). Remove chicken from stock to cooling pan & cool enough to handle. Strain stock and return to stock pot. De-bone chicken & set aside.

For Dumplings - Need
3 C. Unbleached flour
3/4 C. Olive oil
1/2 tsp. salt
1/2 C. cold water
Mix salt & flour in med. mixing bowl. Add oil and work with clean hands to form crumbs that are pea sized. Add water and forms into dough ball.

in Jan Pleasant's handwriting; adapted by Jan Pleasant and Davlyn Walker

Don't work dough too much but enough to have good solid ball. (The more you work it the tougher the dumplins will be :)) Roll out dough with flour into a sheet & cut into strips lengthwise and them cut across to make little squares.

Bring stock back to boil. While boiling add dumplins, few at a time and gently stir to keep separated. Boil about 10 min and add chicken that has been deboned and broken up into small pieces. Then add about 1/4 C heavy cream, and a thickening made from patting 2 tbs. cornstarch into 1 C cold whole milk. Cook until thickened add pepper to taste.

Big Mama's Chili Sauce

Fill a dutch oven with peeled tomatoes. (Do this by dipping fresh tomatoes in boiling water for about one minute until skin spits. It can then be removed when cool.) For this relish you need only the pulp. Pour off all juice and save to can as tomato juice. Add 3-4 coarsely chopped onions, one c. vinegar, 4 c. sugar, 1tbs. Salt, 2tsp black pepper, 1 tsp chili powder. Add 2 coarsely chopped poblano peppers and 1 chopped sweet green pepper. (Poblano peppers are an adaptation made by Jan Pleasant, daughter of Tommie Melton Akin) Cook on medium heat for about four hours until very thick. Seal in pint jars.

Big Mama's Chicken and Dressing

1 boiled chicken, deboned
12 c. yellow cornbread, crumbled
3 c. biscuits, crumbled
2 c. chopped celery
1 large chopped yellow onion
½ bunch chopped green onion
1 Tbsp. salt
1 Tbsp. pepper
1 tsp. poultry seasoning
6 eggs
1 stick (1/2 c.) melted butter
10 c. chicken broth

Mix in large bowl and pour into large roasting pan. Bake at 350 degrees until set and golden brown.

Big Mama's Cornbread

2c. yellow cornmeal, ¼ c. flour, 1c. buttermilk, ½ tsp. salt, 2 tsp. baking powder, ¼ tsp. soda (to 10 inch iron skillet. Heat oven to 425° . Coat bottom of skillet with oil (Big Mama used bacon drippings) and heat in oven 15- 20 min. Remove skillet and sprinkle corn meal in coated skillet. Pour in cornbread batter and bake for 15- 20 minutes. Remove from oven and immediately turn over on plate.

Big Mama's Eggless Fruitcake (her handwriting)

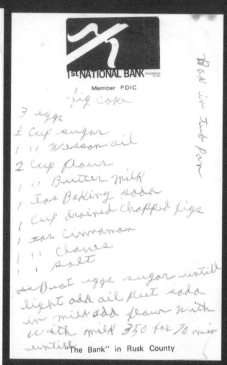

½ tsp each allspice, cinnamon, cloves, and nutmeg. Mix dry ingredients. Cream sugar and butter. Alternate adding milk and dry ingredients while mixing. Stir in raisins, nuts and spices. Bake in 2 greased and floured 8 inch layers at 350 degrees for 20 minutes. Do not over bake. Frost with powdered sugar icing.

Big Mama's Fig Cake (her handwriting)

Big Mama's Greens

A "mess" of greens, turnip and mustar mixed (4 quart Dutch oven)
A 4-6 oz. block Salt pork
About 1 Tbsp. salt
A sprinkle of sugar to cut the sharpne of the greens
Bring to a boil and then turn down to simmer until greens are tender.

Big Mama's Fried Chicken

1 whole chicken cut for frying. Salt chicken pieces and let them sit for a bit. Then place in large bowl and cove in buttermilk. Let it sit for at least 15 minutes. Roll each piece in flour and fry in hot oil (in cast iron skillet).

A Hog Killin' Day

Jan also recalls her mom, Tommie, and Big Mama making sausage. It was   bitter winter and Big Mama and Big Daddy had been given a hog (hog killing was done in the winter so that the pork wouldn't go rancid before it cou be treated and preserved, thus the saying, "It's a hog killin' day" on a cold day). Jan says that she, her sister Lisa, and Tommie rode out to help Big Mama make sausage. When they arrived, Big Mama had everything set up on t back porch and made Tommie sew casings from old sheets and pillowcases while Big Mama hand ground the po and stuffed the casings. Jan says that what she remembered the most about that day was how extremely cold it wa and the nostalgia of the hand made goods.

Big Mama's Homemade Rolls
(Auntie's handwriting)

Best Home Made Rolls

1 Cake or pkg. of yeast dissolved
in ¼ C Warm water.
2/3 Cup Butter (oleo)
½ C. Sugar
1 teaspoon Salt
1 Cup mashed potatoes
1 Cup Scalded Sweet Milk
2 eggs - well beaten
Flour to make a dough
4 Cups or more
Melt butter & add to scalded
Milk - next add sugar & salt
Let Cool to lukewarm —
Add eggs, potatoes yeast & flour
You have added enough Flour
When it is hard to Stir —
Turn on board & knead — add
Flour until it wont stick to board
This May be put in Box
over

and used later.
To use at once let dough
rise until double in bulk.
Shape — let rise again
until light —
Bake 400°

Jewish Coffee Cake
(Tommie's handwriting)

Jewish Coffee Cake

2 cups Sugar
2 Sticks Butter
2 Eggs
3 Cups Flour
2 Teaspoons Baking Powder
½ cup of nuts
1 Teaspoon Vanilla
1 Large can Pet milk
1 8 oz. Bottle cherries

Cream butter, sugar & eggs.
Fold in dry ingredients alt. with
milk. Add nuts & cherries.
Bake in tube pan at 350° 1 hr.

Big Mama's Hot Water Cornbread

2 c. white corn meal
2 Tbsp.s baking powder
2 tsp.s of salt
Boiling water at a rolling boil
10" Cast iron skillet of about ¼" oil, heated to
about 325 degrees- 350 degrees

Mix dry ingredients together and make a well in
the mixture. Slowly pour a boiling water and mix.
Continue until the mixture is thick enough to make
stiff patties that show finger indentions when patted
(Tommie says to have a bowl of cold water available
to be able to cool hands in between forming patties). Lay patties in the hot grease and fry until they
are golden. Makes about (10) 2 ½ inch cornbread
patties.

Big Mama's Lime Pickles

8 lbs. sliced cucumbers
2 c. pickling lime
2 gal. water
2 qt. vinegar
9 c. sugar
2 Tbs. salt
1/2 box pickling spices

Put cucumbers in mixture of lime and water in enamel or pottery or crockery container. They will need to
soak in lime water for 24 hours. Drain and wash thoroughly through 3 cold water rinses. Mix vinegar, sugar,
salt and pickling spices in large cooking kettle. Add cucumbers and let stand for 3 hours; bring to boil and
cook for 30 minutes. Put in hot jars and seal.

Big Mama's New Potatoes with Cream Sauce

For a 2 quart pot: Scrub, salt, and boil new potatoes. Put about 2 heaping Tbsp.s flour to ½ c. milk and stir vigorously with a fork to remove all lumps (Tommie shakes it in a jar). Pour over boiling potatoes (as they are done). Turn off burner, add about ½ stick of butter, pepper to taste and let stand on warm burner until ready to serve.

Big Mama's Pound Cake

3 c. Sugar
4 eggs
1 c. Crisco or butter
¼ tsp salt
¼ tsp soda
1 c. buttermilk
1 Tbsp water
3 c. flour (sifted at least 3 times)
1 Tbsp flavoring (any flavor) (Big Mama always used Watkin's Butternut or Vanilla)

Cream sugar and Crisco. Add eggs one at a time, beating after each one. Sift dry ingredients and add alternately with buttermilk. Add water and flavor. Bake at 350 degrees for one hour and twenty-five minutes.

Big Mama's Peach Cobbler (Tommie's Handwriting)

Mamma's Peach Cobbler

Batter:
1 cup sugar
1 cup flour
1/2 teaspoon baking powder
1/8 teaspoon salt
2/3 cup milk

Mix together

Filling:
2 cups sliced peaches
(need to be juicy but you may add a little water)
1/2 cup sugar
Mix sugar with peaches
Then melt 1 stick of butter
in baking pan. Pour in
batter. Pour peach mixture
on top. Bake at 350° for 25-30
minutes.
Best served with vanilla Ice Cream

Big Mama's Plain Cake (Tommie's handwriting)

Plain Cake

1 c. shortening
2 c. sugar
1/2 teaspoon salt
1/2 teas. soda
1/2 tea Baking Powder
4 eggs
1 c. buttermilk
2 tlbs. lemon extract
3 cups all purpose Flour

Place all ingredients in
mixing bowl. Beat 3
min. Bake in tube
pan for 1 hr. at 325°
Remove from oven
Loosen around edge of
pan with knife & then
pour the following over
the cake: 1 1/2 cups sifted
powdered sugar 5 talbs
of orange juice 5 tlbs
of lemon juice. Return
to oven & leave 3 mins
Turn onto plate. Turn
top side up inverterto

Kathryn, Sandy, Tommie, Big Mama, Maxine Maxwell (neighbor) and Patsy

Big Mama's Sweet Potato Pie

3 c. mashed sweet potatoes
2 eggs beaten
1 c. sugar
1 small can Pet milk
1 tsp. vanilla
½ tsp. nutmeg
½ stick butter
1 unbaked pie shell
Mix all together and pour into pie shell. Bake at 350 degrees for approx. 45 min.

Big Mama's Syrup Pudding (Tommie's handwriting)

Left to right: Mandy Hancock, Big Mama, and Gina Ryan Dodge

> Syrup Pudding
> 1 Cup of Hot water
> Blend Crisco & Sugar
> 1 cup crisco
> 2/3 cup sugar.
> 2 Teaspoons ginger.
> 2 teaspoons soda.
> 3 cups flour.
> pinch of salt
> 1 Cup syrup
> 3 eggs
> Cream Crisco & sugar
> add eggs.

Blend Crisco and sugar. Add eggs and syrup (ribbon cane, sorghum, or molasses). Mix spices, salt, and flour and add to mixture. Add hot water. Bake in a greased skillet until set.

Big Mama's Uncooked Fruit Cake (Tommie's handwriting)

Left to right: Mike Stokley, Big Mama, Pat, Hansel; Left to right, holding boxes: Jan, Lisa, Dewayne; Left to right, front: Betty, Charlie, June, Harold, and Tommie, holding Stacy.

> Uncooked Fruit Cake
> 1 lb. hot vanilla wafer
> 1 can E. Brand milk
> 1 lb. pecans, chopped
> 1 hot Raisins
> 1 lb. candied cherries
> (½ lb. each red & green)
> Vanilla

Mix in the order of ingredients and put in buttered loaf pan (sometimes Big Mama added coconut to the mixture).

Big Mama's White Cake
(her handwriting)

Please use this scratch pad instead of our counter checks
THANK YOU

White cake

2 cup sugar

2 " crisco

1/4

1 pinch salt

3 cup flour

3 Teas Baking Powder

3 eggs whites

1 1/2 cup milk

1 Tea vanilla

CITIZENS NATIONAL BANK OF HENDERSON
(ask for new supply when needed)

Sift dry ingredients and set aside. Cream sugar and Crisco; alternately add milk and dry ingredients to creamed mixture; add vanilla. Fold in beaten egg whites. Bake in two 8 inch payer pans or in one 9x13 inch pan.

Big Mama baked a coconut cake every Christmas. Traditionally, Big Daddy's job was to crack the fresh coconut. Big Mama used this recipe to make her coconut cakes (in layers) and used Seven Minute frosting to ice them. She grated the fresh coconut and sprinkled it on the outside of the cake. See Kathryn's section for frosting.

Big Mama's Yeast Biscuits
(Auntie's handwriting)

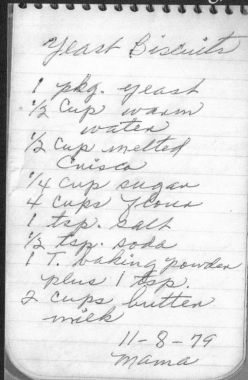

Yeast Biscuits

1 pkg. yeast

1/2 cup warm water

1/2 cup melted Crisco

1/4 cup sugar

4 cups flour

1 tsp. salt

1/2 tsp. soda

1 T. baking powder plus 1 tsp.

2 cups butter milk

11-8-79

Mama

Big Mama's Whole Cranberry Sauce

1c. water
1c. sugar
3c. fresh or frozen cranberries

Bring water and sugar to a boil in a medium saucepan. Add cranberries and return to a boil. Reduce heat and boil for ten minutes, stirring occasionally. Pour sauce into a bowl, cover, and cool completely at room temperature before refrigerating until time to serve.

Glenda, Mandy and Big Mama

Selfish? ME?

I was born the first of seven grandchildren to Harold Rayford and Tommie Jean Melton Akin (Poppy and Grammie). My mother, Jan, was their oldest daughter. When I was born, my mother and father lived on Pine Street in Henderson, Texas. Our house was about three houses down the street from Big Mama's. Big Mama was my great- grandmother and the affectionate mother to my Grammie and six more daughters. There was Auntie (Frances), Aunt Dot (Dorothy), Aunt June, Aunt Betty, Aunt Kat (Kathryn), Aunt Pat, and Grammie. At the time when I was born, Aunt Betty and Uncle Charles were up visiting Big Mama (they lived in the Houston area).

We only lived in that rent house for 2 years, yet I have vague memories of visiting Big Mama's during that time and many memories of her after we moved. I remember her Oil of Olay lotion and smooth skin which always smelled of roses. I recall that she ate Roman Meal bread and that she was faithful to her daytime soap operas.

My cousin Glenda (Aunt Pat's daughter), also stayed with Big Mama a lot. She recalls one time when I was really young and my mother informed Big Mama that she would not be having any more children. Big Mama responded, "Well Jan, then you're gonna have to teach her how to not be selfish."

Frances Elizabeth
MeltonBertram

Photo by Rebecca Haskell

Auntie's Gardenias
20"x35"
Acrylic paint, gold leaf, grave rubbing, and faux pearls on wooden panel

I went to see Auntie in the assisted living facility (Emeritus House) last Tuesday (September 4, 2012). We had a great visit. We always do. I feel very connected to Auntie. I believe it is her independent spirit and her joyful heart. For as long as I have known her, her eyes have smiled. And that always makes my heart smile.

During our visit I asked her what domestic art she missed the most. She told me "cooking and gardening." Then I asked what her favorite flower was that she liked to grow. She told me that it was gardenias. I should have guessed her answer to the question, given that, among all of the recipes Auntie gave me to look through for this cookbook, she had included this recipe for ridding gardenia bushes of the yellow on their leaves.

Outside the window of Auntie's room, she has several bird feeders. She has my Aunt Pat come fill the feeders so that she can watch the birds. When I go to take Bella (my dog) to see Auntie, the highlight of Bella's trip is to climb in Auntie's lap while she is in her recliner, and watch the birds. In observing Bella's pleasure in the event, I think to myself, "If watching those birds feeding warms that little dog's heart so much, then how much more joy must it bring to Auntie?" She may not be able to nurture a garden or nourish others with her cooking, but she can feed the birds who never worry about from where their food comes. No wonder Auntie's eyes are always smiling.

Born: May , 1920
Married: Cleburn Moore
Married: Bill Wells
Married: Don Bertram
Step- Children: Patsy Medley and O'Dell Wells

*All of Frances's recipes are in her own handwriting

Auntie's Coconut Pecan Frosting

Coconut & Pecan
Frosting
1 1/3 C. evaporated milk
1 1/3 C. sugar
4 egg yolks, beaten
2/3 C. margarine
1 1/2 tsp. Vanilla
1 1/3 C. Coconut
1 1/3 C. chopped pecans
Combine milk, sugar,
egg yolks and oleo in
heavy saucepan,

bring to a boil,
and cook over medium
heat 12 min. stirring
Constantly. Add
vanilla, coconut
and pecans. Stir
till Cool and of
spreading consistency.
3 1/2 cup

Auntie's Best Pecan Pie

The Best Pecan
Pie
1 stick Oleo
1 Cup light
Karo
1 cup sugar
3 lg. eggs, beaten
1/2 tsp. lemon
juice
1 tsp. Vanilla
dash of salt
1 cup Chopped
pecans
8 or 9 inch un-
baked pie shell

Brown Oleo in
saucepan till
golden brown,
do not burn.
Cool. In separate
bowl add ingred-
ients in order
listed; stir.
Blend in browned
Oleo well. Pour
in pie shell
and bake 425° for
10 min. then 325°
for 40 minutes.
Very Good
F.E.B.

Auntie's Flaky Pastry

Flaky Pastry
needs no chilling
2 C. Flour
1 tsp. salt
2/3 C. Crisco
2 T butter or
   Oleo
   -melted
5 T. Cold water
1 tsp. sugar
1/4 tsp. Cream
   of tartar
1 T. Vinegar
Mix well Flour
and salt. Cut in
Crisco and

Oleo until ~~coarse~~
coarse crumbs.
add water and
Vinegar, mixing
with fork.
Form in ball.
Roll out. Lift
to pie plate
(pastry is tender
and may tear)
Makes 2 Crust
8 or 9 inch pie
shells.
          T. E. B.
          11-25-79
(Very Good)

Auntie's Fantasy Fudge

Fantasy Fudge

3 C. sugar
1/4 C. Oleo
5 1/3 oz. Can milk
1 - 12 oz. pkg.
   semi-sweet
   Chocolate pieces
1 - 7 oz. jar marsh-
   mallow Cream
1 C. Chopped nuts
1 tsp. Vanilla
Combine sugar,
Oleo and milk
in heavy 2 1/2 qt.
sauce pan,
bring to a full
rolling boil,

stirring Constantly.
Boil 5 min. over
med. heat stir-
ring Constantly
to prevent
scorching. Re-
move from
heat; stir in
Chocolate until
melted. add
marshmallows,
nuts and Vanilla;
beat till well
blended. Pour
in greased 13 X 9
in. pan. Cool.
Cut in squares.
Makes 3 lbs.
          10-24-76

Auntie's Icicle Pickle's

Frans Icicle Pickles

3 lbs. 4 in. Cucumbers
6 small Onions
6-5 in. pieces Celery
1 T. mustard
1 qt. Spear vinegar
1/4 cup salt
2 -1/2 cups sugar
1 cup water
   Wash Cucumbers, cut length -

to thin slices; soak in ice wa
to 5 hours. Drain and pack in
int jars. add 1 quartered onion
piece Celery, and 1/2 teaspoon mus
nd seed to each jar. Combine v
gar, salt, sugar, and water. Bri
boil. Pour solution over Cucumbe
ll jars to within 1/2 in. of tops. Se
yield 6 pints.
   I sometimes add garlic, dill and
sh pepper pod.   Frances Bertram
                    aug. 22 - 1976

Auntie's Homemad Saurkraut

omeade Sauerkraut

5 lb. Cabbage finely
     shredded.
3 1/2 T. Pickling Salt

   soil Cabbage and
salt in large pan.
Stir well.
   Pack Cabbage tight
in pint jars. Leave
1/2 in. headspace.
Fill jars with Cold
water, leave 1/2 in.
headspace. Cover
with metal lids, and
screw bands tight.
   Let ferment at room
temp. for 3 to 4 days.
a small amount
of liquid will escape)
   Wash outside of jars,
screw bands tight.
Process in boiling-
water bath for
15 min. yield 5 pts.
   To serve rinse
sauerkraut well,
squeeze out liquid
for each pt. heat
2 T. bacon fat in
skillet. add kraut
and fry 10 min.

Frances at her place in Overton

Auntie's Oatmeal Muffins

Oatmeal Muffins

1 1/4 C. boiling water
1/2 tsp. salt
1 C. Oats (un-
    Cooked)
1/2 C. Oleo
1 C. firmly packed
    brown sugar
1 C. sugar
2 eggs
1 1/3 C. self-rising
    flour
1 tsp. Cinnamon
1 1/2 C. Coconut
    Combine water

salt & Oats, let
stand 20 min.
Cream Oleo and
sugar, add eggs
and beat well.
Combine flour &
Cinnamon, add to
creamed mixture.
Add coconut &
Oat mixture,
stir well. Bake
in muffin pans
350° for 25 min.
Makes 2 dz.
            10-24-76
            F.E.B.

Auntie's Own Season Salt Mix

My Own Seasoned
Salt Mix

1 C. salt
2 1/2 tsp. paprika
2 tsp. dry mustard
1 1/2 tsp. Oregano
1 tsp. garlic salt, or
    garlic powder, to
    taste
1/2 tsp. Onion powder
    Mix and store in
air tight Container.
Makes 1 Cup.
            12-23-79
            F.E.B.

Auntie's Gardenia Treatment

For Yellow
Leaves on
Gardenias

Mix 1 heaping
tablespoon
Epsom Salts
in one 1/2 gallon
of water
Spray on
leaves and
let run onto
ground around
plants
            8-30-77

Auntie's Window Cleaner

Window Cleaner

1 pint 70% rubbing
    alcohol
1/2 Cup sudsy
    ammonia
1 teaspoon dish
    detergent and
enough water to
make a gallon
in all.
    Very good.
            1992

40 SCHOOL DAYS 41

Left to right: Frances, Kathryn, Dorothy holding Patsy, June, and Betty

Crybox Funeral

According to Frances, the older girls (who were herself, Dorothy, June, and Betty) were given baby dolls for Christmas one year. They were the kinds of dolls which cried when moved. Annoyed by the crying, the young girls (prompted by Dorothy, the known instigator), the girls removed the cry boxes from the dolls. They proceeded to bury the boxes, holding a funeral for them. Needless to say, when Big Mama discovered what they had done, they were made to dig the boxes back up and re-insert them in the dolls.

Left to right: Dorothy, Kathryn, Frances, Meredith (cousin), June, and Betty

Under the Sycamore tree at the Minden, TX homeplace

Left to right: Frances, Dorothy, June, Betty, Kathryn, Patsy, and Tommie

Dorothy Rae
Melton Akin

Photo by Rebecca Haskell

Aunt Dot's Lime Pickles
20"x17"
Acrylic paint, gold leaf, grave rubbing, and faux pearls on wooden panel

"Big Mama was always big on pickle making. She used to make amazing peach pickles that were so sweet and spicy with cinnamon & cloves. She also made a sweet cucumber pickle called lime pickles. They acquired this name because they had to soak overnight in pickling lime to make them crisp.

I remember a time in my young adulthood when I lived on Pine St. in Henderson two doors down from Big Mama. Aunt Dot had come for a few days to help Big Mama make those pickles. I remember Aunt Dot sitting at the dining room table that was in the kitchen, slicing cucumbers into a big crock churn (formerly Big Mama's butter churn) for them to sit in lime overnight.

The next day the spicy smell of those pickles permeated that small house. That smell today, when I make those same pickles, reminds me of those wonderful family times."

- Jan Akin Pleasant

Born: July 21, 1922
Married: Millard Akin
Children: Sandy Akin White, Sherry Akin Vein, Marla Akin Bracewelll, Phillip Akin, and Nyla Akin Dalhaus
Died: 2009

Dorothy's Banana Cake
from Aunt Mary
(her handwriting)

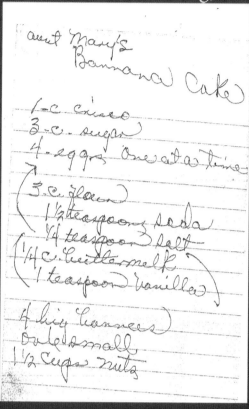

Dorothy's Coconut Cake

1 package yellow cake mix
1-4 serving size instant vanilla pudding and pie filling
1 1/3 c. water
4 eggs
¼ c. oil
2 c. flaked coconut
1 c. chopped walnuts or pecans

Blend cake mix, pudding mix, water, eggs, and oil in large bowl. Beat at medium speed for 4 minutes. Stir in coconut and nuts. Pour into 3 greased and floured 9" pans. Bake at 350 degreesfor 35 min. Cool in pans for about 15 min. Remove and cool on wire rack. Fill and frost with coconut cream cheese frosting.

Frosting:

4 Tbsp. butter
2 c. flaked coconut
(1) 8 oz. pkg. cream cheese
2 tsp. milk
3 ½ c. sifted powdered sugar
½ tsp. vanilla

Melt 2 Tbsp. butter in a skillet. Add coconut. Stir constantly over low heat until golden brown. Spread coconut on paper towel to cool. Cream 2 Tbsp. butter with cream cheese, adding milk and sugar alternately, beating well. Add vanilla and stir in 1 ¾ c. of the toasted coconut. Mix and spread between layers and on sides of the cake. Sprinkle remaining coconut all over the cake.

Dorothy's Chipped Beef

16 oz. (1 lb.) shaved beef
½ stick butter
2 heaping Tbs. Flour
½ c to begin (add more to correct consistency)

Melt butter in a cast iron skillet add flour and stir until dissolved but don't let flour brown. Add milk and stir with a wire whisk to dissolve all clumps. Stir to the consistency of buttermilk or yogurt. Add beef salt and pepper do taste.

Dorothy and Sandy

"Dorothy Rae Melton Akin. Second daughter of Sample and Pearl; wife of Millard Marvin Akin; mother of five lucky children; Mama Dot to eight grandchildren and Aunt Dot to many adoring nieces and nephews. Everyone loved 'Dot.'

Mama was comfort, knowledge, peace, and love. I guess that is why she didn't bat an eye when I decided I would be a hippie when I was 15.

Mama was the original multi-tasker. She could cook, sew, garden, paint anything, wallaper, mow, kill chickens, drink a beer, dance, doctor a dog, and look good in a hat. We all loved her cooking. She made the BEST cornbread dressing in the world and no one turned down her chipped beef and gravy over toast or biscuits, rice, or a wooden shingle.

She made almost all of mine and Nyla's clothes all through school. I would pick fabric and patterns and away she would go. SWEET! I had so many cute outfits.

Mama always dressed up, put on lipstick and hairspray when she left the house. She taught us the importance of good manners, etiquette, and respecting our elders. Dot and Daddy raised five children born over a span of 17 years and I believe were able to give each one of us just what we needed for a happy and contented life."

- Marla Akin Bracewell

39 SCHOOL DAYS 40

Dorothy's Carrot Salad

2 lb. sliced, cooked carrots (not soft)
1 sliced bell pepper
1 large onion sliced into rings
¾ c. sliced celery
1 small can sliced ripe olives
1 can water sliced chestnuts

Marinate in the following blended mixture:
1 can tomato soup
1 c. sugar
1 c. oil
¾ c. apple cider vinegar
1 tsp. salt
1 tsp. dry mustard
1 Tbsp. Worcestershire sauce

Keeps well for up to 2 weeks in refrigerator when tightly covered.

Dorothy's Delight

1-12 oz. bag of chocolate or butter-scotch chips
1 c. cocktail peanuts
1 ½ c. chow mein noodles
½ c. raisins (optional)

Melt chips in double boiler. Cool to room temperature and add nuts, noodles, and raisins. Drop on wax paper to cool.

Dorothy's Heavenly Hash

4 eggs
2 c. sugar
2 sticks melted butter
1 ½ c. self-rising flour
4 Tbsp. cocoa
1 c. chopped pecans
2 tsp. vanilla
1 16 oz. bag mini marshmallows

Beat eggs slightly, stir in sugar and then butter. Mix flour, cocoa, and nuts in a
separate bowl. Make a well in the dry
ingredients, add in egg mixture, and stir evenly. Pour into a greased and floured 13x9 inch cake pan. Bake at 325 degrees for 35-45 minutes or until inserted tooth-pick comes out clean. When cake is done, while it is still hot, cover with marshmallows. Let cool and poor icing over the marshmallow covered cake.

Icing:
4 Tbsp. melted butter
½ c. canned cream
4 Tbsp. cocoa
1 box powdered sugar
Mix until creamy. Pour over cake. Cake is better if it is let to stand overnight.

Dorothy's Hummingbird Cal

3 c. flour
1 tsp. salt
1 tsp. soda
1 tsp. cinnamon
2 c. sugar
3 eggs, beaten
1 ½ c. vegetable oil
1 ½ tsp. vanilla
(1) 8oz. can crushed pineapple, undrained
2 c. chopped bananas
2 c. chopped nuts (divided)

Combine dry ingredients in a larg
mixing bowl. Add eggs and oil and
stir until moistened. Stir in vanilla
pineapple, bananas, and 1 c. of nut
Spoon batter into three greased an
floured pans and bake at 350
degrees for 25-30 minutes or until
an inserted toothpick comes out
clean. Cool in pans on a wire rack
for about 10 minutes. Then remove
cake from pans and cool complete

While cake is baking, make frostin
(2) 8 oz. pkg. softened cream chees
1 c. softened butter
2- 16 oz. boxes powdered sugar
2 tsp. vanilla

Combine cream cheese and butter, creaming until smooth. Add sugar, beating until light and fluffy. Stir in vanilla. Ice cake between layers and around the cake. Sprinkle the remaining chopped nuts on cake.

Dorothy's Meringue Cookies

2 egg whites beaten stiff
2/3 c. sugar
1 c. chopped nuts
1 c. chocolate chips

Preheat oven to 350 degrees. Fold the sugar, nuts, and chips into the egg white mixture. Drop dollops on foil covered cookie sheet. Turn off the oven when ready to put in the oven. Let set in the oven for 4-8 hours, letting dry.

Dorothy's Orange Candy Cake

1 c. butter
4 eggs
4 c. sifted flour
1 Tbsp. grated orange rind
1 small package finely chopped dates
1 lb. finely chopped orange candy slices
2 c. pecans
1 1/3 c. buttermilk
1 tsp. soda
2 c. sugar

Cream butter with sugar and eggs, one at a time. Mix soda in buttermilk. Add flour alternately with buttermilk mixture. Add orange rind, dates, candy, and pecans. Bake in a large greased and floured tube pan at 325 degrees for 1 hour and 45 min. While it is still hot and in the pan, slit cake so that glaze will seep through.

Boil and pour glaze over hot cake:
1c. sugar
½ c. orange juice

Left to Right, standing
Dorothy and Sandy
Left to Right, sitting:
Melvin (Grandpa)
Cooper holding Denise
White, and Pearl

Mama's Pinto Beans

1 lb dry pinto beans
1 bell pepper - chopped
1 onion - chopped
garlic (to taste)
salt (to taste)
salt pork or bacon ends & pieces
chili powder (to taste)

Wash & sort beans. Cover with water, bring to a boil. Turn off and let sit 15 minutes. Turn back on add all ingredients and cook on low boil until beans are tender. Add HOT water as necessary.

This recipe is how Mama taught me to, make pinto beans! Must have hot water cornbread to go with them! hee hee ☺

Dorothy's Molasses Sugar Cookies
(Sandy's handwriting)

Recipe for: Molasses Sugar Cookies
From the Kitchen of: Mom & Mama Hot

3/4 cup shortening
1 cup sugar
1/4 cup molasses
1 egg
2 cups sifted flour
1/2 t. cloves   2 t. soda
1/2 t. ginger
1/2 t. salt
1 t. cinnimon

Melt shortening, let cool. Add sugar molasses & egg. Beat well. Sift together flour, soda, cloves, ginger cinnimon & salt. Add to first mixture. Mix well. Chill. Form in 1 inch balls, roll in granulated sugar & place on greased cookie sheet 2 inches apart. Bake at 375° 8-10 minutes.

KISSIN' KEEPS ME COOKIN'

March 21st

Got your letter today. Had one
written to you but am out of
stamps again. Intended sending it
by your Daddy but forgot.

Was glad to hear you all got
a TV. I know it will help pass
a lot of time. Especially at night.
Sorry to hear about Bettie's baby.
Hope he is OK now.

Got a letter from Mom today too
& she said she hoped she + [?]
could work in here the first.

Ray was home for a few days.
It's raining again here. I'll be so
glad when it stops + everything
is dry again.

I'll go now + get busy.

Pork Chop Casserole
Cover bottom of pan with rice
Cover rice with water unless you
use minute-rice; if so no water
Lay pork chops in + slice an

Dorothy (left) and a friend at her home in Oakland, California, where Millard was stationed in the Air Force.

Left to right: Sandy Akin White, Dorothy and Denise White.

I'm not sure of the date (year) this
letter and the recipe was written. I'm
guessing it was 1958.
Mama and family lived in California,
we lived in Nederland.

The Daisy Bradford Well of 1930:

Frances recalls Big Mama packing a picnic lunch and she and Big Daddy loading them up and going to see the well come in. At that time, there was only Auntie, Dot, June, Betty, and Kat (who was just two years young). They had heard that the well was predicted to erupt that day. Auntie says that it must have been on a Sunday because Big Daddy was off of work. She remembers that the sight was unbelievable: all those men dancing in that slick, black oil.

Also, on display at the East Texas Oil Museum in Kilgore, TX is a wagon belonged to Birdwell Cooper, Pearl's brother. It was donated by Pearl's father, James M. Cooper. Original Cooper land was said to be mere acres from gaining land royalties.

eft to Right, back row: Betty, Frances, Big Mama, and athryn Left to Right, front row: Patsy and Tommie

Left to right: June, Patsy, Frances, Tommie, Big Mama, Big Daddy, Betty

Nila June
Melton Stokley

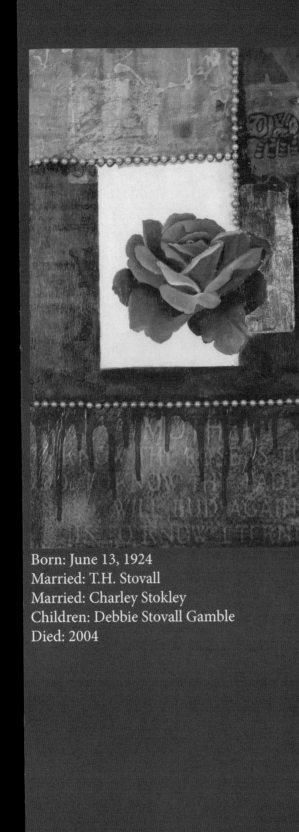

Born: June 13, 1924
Married: T.H. Stovall
Married: Charley Stokley
Children: Debbie Stovall Gamble
Died: 2004

Photo by Rebecca Haskell

Aunt June's Coral Rose
20"x17"
Acrylic paint, gold leaf, grave rubbing, and faux pearls on wooden panel

Aunt June, as most of the sisters, always smiled. I loved to see her wide smile and jovial chuckle. Grammie says that she was always telling a joke, but what I heard her talk about more than anything were her grandchildren, Melanie and Jay Gamble. Aunt June only had one daughter and only two   grandchildren. They were the lights of her heart and the true reason that I believe Aunt June always smiled.

I never saw Aunt June when she wasn't at Aunt Pat's house. They were very close. Aunt June lived in Henderson and worked at the same bank (Henderson First National) together. When Aunt June went into assisted living, Aunt Pat was the sister who attended to her (as she currently does with Auntie). Of course, Aunt June greatly depended on her daughter, Debbie Gamble. Debbie tells me that Aunt June was notorious for giving her recipes and then asking her to prepare them.

In true Melton sister fashion, Aunt June was a marvelous cook. Even in the light of her cooking skills, however, nothing could compare to her green thumb. Debbie tells me that when she had a plant that was barely hanging onto its weak little life, she could send it to Aunt June who would nurse it back to health and make it a thrive.

Among all of Aunt June's plants were her favorite, the coral rose. She loved this beautiful plant. She was drawn to its color, its scent, its feel. Knowing her affinity for this flower, I believe that she felt akin to it in. As her great niece, I imagine that Aunt Junes her own life in the blossoms of the coral rose. It was a beautiful, delicate living being, as her own life had been.

June's Banana Pudding

Banana Pudding

1 lg box vanilla instant pudding
8 oz cream cheese
8- oz Cool Whip
2 cups milk
1 can eagle brand
4 bananas
Vanilla wafers

Mix pudding and milk until thickened. Cream cheese, add
eagle brand - fold into pudding. Layer wafers, bananas, and
pudding. Top with cool whip.

40 SCHOOL DAYS 41

June's Bread Pudding
(Debbie's handwriting)

Bread Pudding
1/2 st. marg.
2 C milk
1 1/2 C sugar
3 eggs
vanilla
cinnamon
9 slices bread

350° abt. 40 min.

June's Blueberry Muffins

1 egg
1/2 c. milk
1/4 c. vegetable oil
1 1/2 c. flour
1/2 c. sugar
2 tsp. baking powder
1/2 tsp salt
1 c. fresh or frozen blueberries

Beat egg with fork and stir in milk and oil. Mix dry
ingredients. Stir together just until flour is moistened.
Batter will be lumpy. Carefully stir in blueberries. Bake
in greased muffin c. 20-25 minutes at 400 degrees.

June's Blueberry Pound Cake

BLUEBERRY POUND CAKE

2 C SUGAR
¾ C BUTER – SOFTENED
6 OZ CREAM CHEEZE
2 OZ ALMOND PASTE

ALL ROOM TEMP – CREAM TIL FLUFFY

4 EGGS   ADD 1 AT TIME

1 ½ C FLOUR
1 ½ t BAKING POWDER
½ t SALT
ADD TO MIX ON LOW

1 ¾ C FROZEN BLUEBERRIES – DRAIN – OR CAN USE CANNED

BAKE 45 MINUTES TO 1 HOUR ON 350

GLAZE

2C POWDERED SUGAR
2T LEMON JUICE
2 T MILK

GLAZE WHEN SLIGHTLY WARM

June's Chicken
(her handwriting)

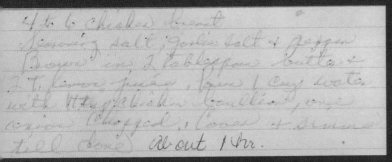

June's Chocolate Fudge (12/22/53)

1 large can evaporated milk
1 jar marshmallow cream
¼ lb. Oleo
(3) 10 oz. pkg. Chocolate chips
5 c. sugar
2 c. Nuts
dash salt
1 tsp vanilla

Mix milk, sugar, oleo, and salt. Boil 6 minutes
stirring constantly. Remove from heat. Add
chocolate chips, marshmallow cream, flavoring
and nuts. Beat well and pour into buttered dish.
Makes 5lbs.

June's Congealed Salad
(her handwriting)

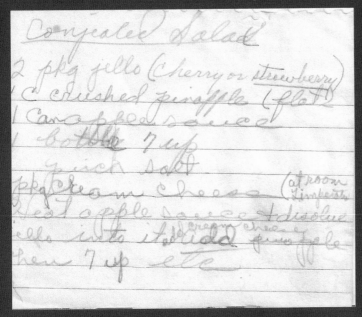

June and T.H. Stovall

June's Cranberry Salad

1 can whole or smooth cranberry sauce
2 small pkgs. Lemon gelatin
(1) 16 oz. can crushed pineapple
1 c. chopped pecans or walnuts
1 c. chopped celery

Heat cranberry sauce with gelatin and stir
until gelatin is dissolved. Cook slightly,
then add the rest of the ingredients. Add
red food coloring if desired. Pour into a
7"x11" casserole dish, a nice bowl, or a 4 c.
mold. Chill until set. Serves 7-8.

June's Fudge Nut Cake
(her handwriting)

Fudge Nut Cake

½ c butter
1 c sugar
2 eggs
1 c flour
4 T cocoa
Salt
1 t van
1 c nuts

Bake mod. oven. Let
Cool + pour fudge icing
over it in pan + Cut
in squares

Icing

2 c sugar
4 T cocoa
1 T corn Syrup
¾ c evap. milk
1 t van
½ c butter (1 sti
Cook t soft ball
Add butter
Cool
Beat

June and Charlie Stokley

June's Fruit Salad
(Debbie's Handwriting)

Fruit Salad

1 can peach pie filling
1 can fruit for salad
                (drained)
2 apples
2 oranges
2 bananas
  strawberries

June's Hashbrown Casserole

2 lbs. frozen hashbrowns
½ c. melted butter
1 can cream of chicken soup
1 pint sour cream
½ c. chopped onion
2 c. grated cheddar cheese
1 tsp. salt
¼ tsp. pepper
2 c. crushed corn flakes
¼ c. melted butter

Defrost hash browns. Combine the next
seven ingredients and mix with hash
browns. Put all in a 3 quart dish. Sauté the
corn flakes in ¼ c. butter and sprinkle on
mixture. Cover and bake at 350 degrees for
about 40 minutes.

June's Lemon Pound Cake

```
            Lemon Pound Cake
3 Cups of Swans down soft silk cake flour
3 Cups of sugar
1 cup of crisco or two sticks of margarine
4 eggs
1 cup of buttermilk

Mix all ingredients together in mix master.

Then add 2 table spoons of hot water with 1/4
teaspoon of soda. Mix well with other ingred-
ients. Then, add 2 tablespoons of lemon extract.

Cook for 1 hour and 15 minutes
350°.
```

June's Pineapple Coconut Pie
(Debbie's handwriting)

Pineapple-
Coconut
Pie

4 eggs beaten
1 1/2 - 2 C sugar
1/2 st   1/2 C butter
1 8oz crushed
    pineapple
    (unsweet)
1 C coconut
1 T flour
1 T cornmeal
1 t vanilla
350°
    45-50 min.

June's Sand Tarts
(Debbie's handwriting)

Sand Tarts
Bake at 350°
10-15 minutes

2 C flour
1 C butter (soft)
4 T powdered sugar
2 T vanilla
pinch salt
1 C pecans

roll into balls or moon
shape. Bake. Cool
+ roll in powder sugar

- Melanie Gamble McMahon

"About my MawMaw:
I remember being amazed at her ability to recall recipes. (She also
knew the name of every kind of plant & flower and knew how to care
for it. Amazing!) I could ask her if she knew a good recipe for any
type of dish and she could recall in detail a recipe for anything. I can
hear her now... a Tbsp. of this and a tsp. of that. She was a very special
grandmother of many talents and
I am still amazed today."

Betty Sue

Melton Jarrell

Photo by Rebecca Haskell

Aunt Betty's Homemade Peach Ice Cream
20"x17"
Acrylic paint, gold leaf, grave rubbing, and faux pearls on wooden panel

Every sister agrees that Aunt Betty was the best cook of them all (although I can't imagine anyone comparing to any of them). Aunt Betty was the aunt to whom I felt closest. Perhaps it is because she was present at my birth. She and Uncle Charles had come to visit Big Mama (who lived three houses down from the little rent house my parents lived in on Pine Street in Henderson). Mom had gone into labor but the doctors sent her home, telling her that she was not quite ready yet. Knowing that the time would come within the following 24 hours of my Mom being sent home, Aunt Betty told Mom to have Daddy call her when she went back to the hospital. Daddy did just that and Aunt Betty and Grammie were the first of the seven sisters to meet me.

By the time I was three, I knew my nickname from Aunt Betty: "Precious." As I grew to an old 4 years of age, I remember Aunt Betty teaching me some of my nursery rhymes. One went like this:

> Peanut was layin on tha railroad tracks,
> His heart was in a' flutter.
> Along came a jellybean in his Ford,
> and HOTDOG (clap loudly here)! PEANUT BUTTER!

Born: February 2, 1926
Married: Charles Jarrell
Children: Lynn Jarrell, Jo Beth Jarrell Massey, and Bonnie Jarrell Booher
Died: March 2003

The thing about Aunt Betty that everyone loved was that spirit of unconditional love. She gave so freely and this giving is what made her so beautiful. She was the ultimate nurturer. When my Grammie was a child, Aunt Betty took care of her. When family sat down to dinner, everyone had to physically put their hands over their glasses to stop her filling them with tea because she would not sit and eat for taking care of everyone else. She literally filled everyone.

Aunt Betty was most known for two of her recipes: her homemade rolls (which was actually Big Mama's recipe) and her homemade ice cream. When electric ice cream makers became all the rage, Aunt Betty made ice cream weekly for her family, keeping her freezer stocked. On special occasions, especially when she was having company, as my mother recalls when she visited, Aunt Betty made homemade peach ice cream, a recipe to which no other ice cream could compare.

I think all of her nieces and nephews felt her nurture and most of us took something. I know that she gave me a legacy of wanting to be more kind, loving, and unconditional with my nurtuting others. Her legacy reminds me to be a good listener, to look people in the eye and say "I understand" when I am listening. Looking back, I do believe Aunt Betty was partially wrong about one thing: she was the precious one.

Betty's Baked Corn
(Kathryn's handwriting)

Baked Corn   By Betty

1 Egg
1/2 Box Cornbread mix 2 T Sugar
1 onion Chopped   Salt & Pepper
1/2 Stick Butter, oleo   1 C Cream style Corn
    Melt oleo in baking dish & pour the
mixture over Butter & bake 45 MIN 350°

                    Use 8 X 8 dish

Betty's Best Homeade Rolls
(Tommie's handwriting)

Best Home Made Rolls

1 Cake or pkg. of yeast dissoled
  in 1/4 C. warm water
2/3 Cup Butter (oleo)
1/2 C. Sugar
    1 teaspoon Salt
1 Cup mashed potatoes
1 Cup Scalded Sweet Milk
2 eggs - well beaten
Flour to make a dough
4 Cups or more
    Melt butter & add to scalded
Milk - Next add sugar & salt
Let Cool to luke warm -
Add eggs, potatoes yeast & flour
You have added enough flour
When it is hard to Stir -
Turn on board & Knead - add
flour until it wont stick to board
    This may be put in box
                        over

and used later.
    To use at once let dough
rise until double in bulk.
Shape - let rise again
until light -
    Bake 400°

Betty's Blueberry Pie
(Betty's handwriting)

BlueBerry Pie (Betty's)
1 8 oz. block cream cheese
2 package. dream whip
1 box pd. Sugar

Cream cream cheese - beat
pd. Sugar into this & add
whipped dream whip
pour into baked pie
Shell & top, with blueberry
Pie filling   (over)

40 SCHOOL DAYS 41

Betty's Coconut Cream Cake
(Tommie's handwriting)

Betty's 10-15-77
Coconut Cream Cake

1 Box White Cake mix
¼ cup wesson oil
1-8 oz carton Sour cream
1 teaspoon vanilla
1 Can 8 or 9 oz Cream of Coconut
3 eggs
Bake at 350° about 20 min.

Icing
8 oz. cream cheese
1 box pd. sugar
1 teaspoon Vanilla
1 Can Coconut sprinkled over

THANKS FOR USING

SPT SOUTHERN PACIFIC TRANSPORT COMPANY
OF TEXAS AND LOUISIANA
SWT SOUTHWESTERN TRANSPORTATION COMPANY

Betty's Divinity
(from Aunt Mary Cooper in Tommie's handwriting)

Aunt Mary Divinity
2½ cups sugar
½ cup white Karo
½ cup Water
2 egg white (beaten stiff)
1 tsp Vanilla
1 cup nuts
Cook, Water, sugar, & Karo without stirring till spins a thread, pour ½ of syrup (over)

over beaten egg whites beating —
return other half to stove & cook to brick ball stage — Pour over egg whites, add Vanilla & nuts beat until thick —

Lynn Jarrell and Betty Melton Jarrell. At this time, Betty and Lynn were living back in Minden with Big Mama and Big Daddy. Charles was serving in the Marines and active in World War II. Betty is wearing her Marine pin on her left side to honor her husband's service.

Betty at her and Charles's home in Nederland.

Betty's Fruit Salad

4 ½ oz. Pkg Dream Whip
2 cans fruit cocktail drained
1 large can pineapple chunks drained and sliced
1 large bottle salad cherries drained and sliced, reserve
juice
1 oz. pkg. cream cheese
1 small pkg. Miniature marshmallows
Prepare dream whip as directed on package and set aside.
Beat with mixer cream cheese, ¼ c. sugar, cherry juice.
Add fruit and marshmallows. Fold in Dream whip. Spread
in 9 x13 dish and freeze.

Betty's Ice Cream

4 eggs
1c. sugar
1 Tbsp. Vanilla
½ pt. Whipping Cream
2 cans sweetened condensed milk
1 ½ qts. Milk

Beat eggs until thick and lemon
colored. Beat in sugar gradually. Add vanilla. Fold in
whipping cream. Stir in condensed milk.
Pour into ice cream freezer.
Add milk. Freeze in ice cream
freezer according to freezer
directions. Makes 1 Gallon.

Charles and Betty Melton Jarrell

Betty's Frozen Fruit Salad

8 oz. Cool Whip
8 oz. cream cheese softened
¾ c. sugar
10 oz. Package frozen
strawberries
2 bananas
½ c. nuts
1 can chunk pineapple drained
Beat cream cheese and sugar. Add in fruit and nuts. Fold in
Cool Whip. Spread in 9x13 pan and freeze.

Betty's Ginger Cookies
(her handwriting)

Oct 27 '79

Betty Ginger Cookies

1 cup sugar
2/3 shortening Maybe 3/4 cup
2 1/4 cup flour
1/4 cup syrup (Any Kind)
2 teaspoons soda
1 teaspoon Ginger
3/4 teaspoon Cinnimon
1/4 teaspoon Cloves
1 teaspoon salt
1 egg

Cream sugar & short add
egg & beat well, add
syrup & beat a little more,
add dry ingredints and
roll into balls & roll
in sugar & bake at 375
for 80 to 12 mins.

Betty's Gumbo

Gumbo

chicken (1 fryer)
bell pepper (chopped)
can whole tomatoes (reg. size)
can tomato sauce
large onions. chopped
cups flour
cup shortening
qts water or more if desired
cup green onions, chopped
cup parsley, chopped
3 stalks or ribs celery, chopped
3 pods garlic, minced
2 boxes frozen okra, 10 oz size
salt, pepper & tabasco to taste

Make roux in heavy skillet by stirring
flour & shortening until well browned.
Transfer to deep gumbo pot, add
water, tomatoes, sauce & cook five
minutes. Add celery, bell pepper, okra,
onions & garlic & cook 10 min. Then
add parsley, onion tops, & chicken.
Season to taste with salt, pepper,
& tabasco, cook 30 min. longer.
If too thick add more water.

Betty's Ginger Snaps
(June's handwriting)

Betty's Super Ginger Snaps
from June 19_

2 cups flour
3/4 cup Crisco { half of this is butter }
1/2 cup brown sugar
1/2 cup white sugar
3/4 teaspoon each ginger,
   Cinnamon and Cloves
1 egg
1/4 cup light molasses
1 cup finely Chopped nuts
   Cream shortening & butter add
add sugar molasses. Sift spices
with flour, add to creamed mix
add nuts.
   Roll in small balls and
mash with glass in flour.
   Bake 10 to 12 min at 350°

Betty's Pie Crust
(Kathryn's handwriting)

Pie Crust (2 pies)
1 1/2 Sticks oleo (Melted)
1 1/2 Cups flour
1/2 Cup Chopped pecans
3 Tablespoons Sugar
Melt oleo & pour into
flour, pecans & Sugar
& Press into Pans

Big Mama's room at Patsy's House

Back, left to right: Betty, June, Dorothy
Front, left to right: Patsy, Auntie, Big Mama and Tommie

1995 Annual Autumn Hayride and Wienee Roast in Jumbo, Texas

Left to right, back: Mandy Hancock, Lisa Akin Ryan, Patsy and Dorothy
Left to right, front: Betty, Jan Akin Pleasant,
Bonnie Jarrell Booher, and Tommie

Anna Kathryn
Melton Richardson

AND VOTED WIFE AND MOTHER

Photo by Rebecca Haskell

Born: May 13, 1928
Married: Melvin Richardson
Children: Rodger Richardson, Darrell
Richardson, Donna Richardson,
Danny Richardson, and Jo Darlene
Richardson Michalec

Aunt Kat's Mix Master
20"x17"
Acrylic paint, gold leaf, grave rubbing, and faux pearls on wooden
panel

"Our Mother, Anna Kathryn Melton Richardson, is the fifth Pearl
of the Melton Girls. She was born on May 13, 1928. Her birthday
cycles around Mother's Day and Friday 13th! She married Melvin
Richardson on April 10, 1947. Together they brought four children
into their family—Darrell, Donna, Danny and Darlene.

Our childhood was fun, simple and loving. We were lucky to have
a "stay-at-home Mother". She was always there from the first day of
school to the day of graduation – fed, washed, clothed and
disciplined ! Growing up on Garber Lane provided a unique
childhood experience. All the families up and down the street
knew each other and the kids were everywhere. We had a
perfect playground. Mom kept a close eye on not only her children,
but also our playmates. Growing up we always had a clean home,
loving parents and three meals a day – with snacks. Walking was
the norm. There was no second car. If Mom needed to go to the
store we walked – like a mother duck and her ducklings – off we
went.

The common thread through all the Melton girls is food. Boy, can
they cook! Our Mother could turn almost anything into a feast. It
wasn't until years later that I really appreciated all the vegetables
that were forced on us when we were growing up. Beans, peas,
carrots, tomatoes, relish, chow chow and greens were all
abundant. It is really sad that going away to college made me miss
my Mother's cooking. Those visits home were really special for all
of us and the fried chicken, big breakfast and chocolate cake were
very welcomed. One of my favorite simple meals was what she
called S-O-S.

Family gatherings were a big part of the Melton life. My family made many trips
over the years from   Houston to Henderson. Every trip would pull most of the
Melton girls together at Big Mamma's. Now one Melton girl can provide an out-
standing meal, but put several of the sisters in the kitchen at the same time—you
now have a feast! I remember the table in the dining room being covered with
so much food! Years later, I walked through that old farm house before it was
torn down. As a kid it seemed so big. As a young man, it was so small. I don't
know how we all fit in that old dining room. That old farm house on the Laneville
highway provided the best playground for the cousins.

Now at 84, Mom has mastered the fine art of coupon shopping. She can go to
Walmart with a purse full of coupons and no money and return home with food
and change. She has kept us all supplied with toothpaste and soap thanks to
coupons! She has been an inspiration to two of her granddaughters – Margie and
Allison in the fine art of couponing. Donna, Danny, Darlene and I have learned to
be thrifty and to shop for the best deal. Over the years our mother has always been
there for us. Whether it was to babysit, nurse, cook or sew she never complained.
Now with 12 grandchildren and 20 great-grandchildren, life has been good. These
two East Texans, Kat and Mel have carved out a life that has influenced their
children to be responsible, loving and productive stewards of their own families."

Kathryn's Apple Burritos

Apple Burritos

1 Can Apple Pie
1/2 C Water
1 Stick of Butter
1 t. Vanilla

10 flour tortillas
1/2 C Sugar
1 t Cinnamon

Put water, sugar & butter in a sauce pan (Do Not Boil)
Place in 9 x 13 cake pan.
Place 1 or 2 spoonfuls of pie filling in tortilla & roll up.
To warm liquid, add cinnamon & vanilla
Pour mixture over tortillas & push down with spatula.
Bake in oven at 350° for 30 min.
Remove & push down, then cover with foil
Place in oven again for 15 min.

Kathryn's Coconut Layer Cake

2 c. sifted Swans Down Cake Flour
2 tsp. baking powder
½ tsp. salt
2/3 c. butter or other shortening
1 c. sugar

3 egg yolks, well beaten
1/3 c. milk
1 tsp. vanilla
3 egg whites, stiffly beaten
1 can Baker's Coconut, Southern Style

Sift flour once, measure, add baking powder and salt, and sift together three times. Cream butter thoroughly, add sugar gradually, and cream together until light and fluffy. Add egg yolks; then flour, alternately with milk, a small amount at a time. Beat after each addition until smooth. Add vanilla and fold in egg whites. Bake in two greased 9-inch layer pans in moderate oven (375°) 25 to 30 minutes. Spread Seven Minute Frosting between layers and on top and sides of cake. Sprinkle each layer and outside of cake with coconut while frosting is still soft.

Kathryn's Chocolate Frosting
(her handwriting)

Chocolate Frosting
1 Box Powdered Sugar
1/2 cup Crisco
1/4 cup Cocoa
Heat coffee or milk. Use either one. Add enough to make it spreadable.

Kathryn's Cream Cheese Frosting
(her handwriting)

Cream Cheese Frosting
1 8oz Cream cheese   1 tst Vanilla
1 Box Powdered Sugar 1 Stick butter at room temperature.
Cream butter & cream cheese until soft.: Add powdered sugar & Vanilla. Beat well.

Kathryn and Melvin

Kathryn's Dried Pinto Beans
(her handwriting)

Dried Pinto Beans
3 cups dry beans   1 piece of salt pork
1 large onion chopped   a little bacon grease
1 T salt Sugar
Dash of garlic powder
Pick thru the beans & wash well. Add water
& let beans sit overnight. Next morning drain
beans. Add hot water, onions, salt pork, sugar,
& dash of garlic powder. Add salt last 30
min add salt. If liquid is too thin, take about
1 cup beans & mash well, then put back in pot.
If more water is needed, always add hot water.
How to substitute Sweet N'Low for Sugar

	Granulated Sugar			
Sweet 'N Low Packets	1/4c 3 Packets	1/3c 4 Packets	1/2c 6 Packets	1c+8 12 Packets
Sweet 'N Low Bulk	1 tsp	1 1/4 tsp	2 Tsps	4 tsp
Sweet 'N Low Liquid	1 1/2 tsp	2 tsps	1 Tbsp	2 Tbsp

Kathryn's Plantation Gingerbread
(Donna's handwriting)

Kathryn holding Darrell

Kathryn

10-27-97

Plantation Gingerbread

2 1/2 C Flour - Sifted **	1 C Sugar
1 t Baking Soda	3 Eggs
1 1/2 t Ginger	1 C Butter or Oleo - soft
1 t Cinnamon	1 C Light Molasses
1/2 t Nutmeg or Mace	3/4 C Hot Water
1 1/4 t Salt	Sweetened Whipped Cream

Preheat @ 375°. Grease + Flour 13 x 9 x 2 pan.
Sift Flour w/soda, spices + salt; set aside.
In a lg. bowl @ high speed, beat butter,

sugar + eggs until fluffy - about 5 min. On
low speed beat in molasses + hot water. Add
flour mixture, beating til smooth. Turn
batter into prepared pan. Bake in middle own
rack; 35 to 40 mins or until cake tester
comes out clean. Cool partially in pan on
wire rack. Cut into squares while warm.
Serve with whipped cream. Makes 12
servings.

** Sift before measuring

Kathryn's Delicious Gingerbread
(Donna's handwriting)

Grandmothers Delicious Gingerbread

1 C Brown Sugar	2 t Ginger
1 1/2 C Crisco	1 t Cinnamon
2 Eggs	1 1/2 t salt
3/4 C Molasses	1 C buttermilk
2 3/4 C Sifted Flour	2 t Soda

Blend Sugar, Crisco + eggs. Stir in syrup.
Add dry ingredients alternately with
milk; beat well. Pour in greased 13 x 9
pan + bake 350° for 30 - 40 mins.

Kathryn's Meat Loaf

1 lb. ground beef
1 large onion, chopped
1 can of Carnation
evaporated milk
1 green bell pepper, chopped
1 package Lipton Onion Mix
Ketchup to taste (about ¼ c.)
Oatmeal or Cracker Crumbs
(about 3/4 c.)

Mix well and put in baking
dish. Bake at 350 degrees for
about 40 to 45 minutes until
done.

Kathryn's Seven-Minute Frosting

egg whites
½ c. granulated sugar
½ tsp. light corn syrup
/3 c. cold water
/8 tsp. salt
tsp. vanilla

Combine all ingredients except vanilla in top of double boiler. Beat
with mixer on #2 speed until blended, then cook over boiling water
beating constantly on high speed until mixture forms peaks when
beater is raised—about 7 min. Remove from heat. Add vanilla. Beat
n high until spreading consistency, scraping sides—about 2 min.

Kathryn and Darrell

Kathryn's S.O.S.
(Donna's handwriting)

Kathryn's SOS - 1960's
1 lb hamburger meat -
1 Chopped Onion
Salt, Pepper + Oregano

Brown meat; add onions before meat is
fully cooked. Add Salt, pepper + Oregano.
Add flour to Thicken. Add hashbrowns.
Let simmer til hashbrowns get done.
May have to add water til hashbrowns
get done. Eat on Toast.

Potpourri of Memories
by Darrell Richardson

As a Melton cousin, I divide the Melton time line into two eras: Farm house and Town house. The following is a random list of memories from each era.

Farm house:
No paint on the house, smoke house and salted pork, watching the chickens under the house through the cracks in the floor, cold winter night sleeping in the hall bed covered with many blankets, water well on back porch, watching the wasp nest while seated in the outhouse, a trip to the Maxwell's, playing in the barn, eating oats from the feed bin, the gas heaters in the front rooms, screened back porch,the night slop jar, hot summer days and dragon flies, delivering milk with Big Daddy, catalog on out house wall, waking up to the rhythm of Big Mamma's butter churn (chalug-chalug-chalug), hard peaches growing behind the house, playing steam boat on the back porch – cranking the hand crank grinder, sycamore tree in front yard, vintage milk bottles, chiffarobe, no phone, single light bulb in each room, wood floor garage, the smell of manure, being chased by the bull, the old pasture well, pushing the old mower, plants in pots on the porch, zinnias in bloom, the Melton dump, searching for the Guinea hen nest, the pasture across the road, Indian paint brush, butterflies, salted ham in smoke house, bath on the back porch.

Town house:
Pine trees, Pine Street, fall leaves, Big Mama in rocking chair, Saturday night TV, perfectly seasoned vegetables, breakfast, Sunday morning radio, gospel radio quartet, Aunt Louise's Sunday phone call, biscuits from Church's Chicken, furnace in the floor, plants in the bed room, front door never used, snoring, Piggly Wiggley shopping list, fried chicken, potatoes in the leaves by the garage, pound cake rice for breakfast, plants in the living room, full kitchen cabinets, Sunbeam mixer.

At Home in Minden

Left to right: June, Kathryn (on steps), Tommie (hands on her hips), Frances, Betty (holding child), Lynn Jarrell (boy), and Melvin (man squatted)

Left to right: Lynn Jarrel, Kathryn (back turned), Tommie (hands on her hips), Pearl (on porch in front of swing)

Left to right: Frances, Dorothy, June, Betty, Kathryn, Patsy, and Tommie

Patricia Ann
Melton Lee

Photo by Rebecca Haskell

Aunt Pat's Praline Sweet Potatoes
20"x17"
Acrylic paint, gold leaf, grave rubbing, and faux pearls on wooden panel

Aunt Pat has always been the "keeper" of the sisters, so to speak. When Big Mama became too feeble to live alone, Aunt Pat moved her in with her and Uncle Wayne. When Aunt June went into assisted living, Aunt Pat visited her weekly and now that Auntie also lives in an assisted living residence, Aunt Pat visits her every other day. Any time anyone needs to be updated on the family, she is the dispatcher of information, transmitting data from member to member as needed.

Aunt Pat lives in Henderson, where I live now. Although I graduated high school in Carthage (our land and old family farmhouse was just over the Panola County line), I always considered Henderson my home town. I grew up on a track of land which was 19 miles from Carthage, where Grammie lived, and 20 miles from Henderson, where Aunt Pat and Aunt June lived. Because of the close proximity to my own Grandmother, Aunt Pat visited Grammie often, and vice versa. And since I adored those six aunts, any chance I could meet up with them or go with my grandmother, I would.

Born: May 13, 1934
Married: Hansel Walker
Married: Wayne Lee
Children: Dewayne Walker
and Glenda Walker Simmons

The most memorable occasions of gatherings among the sisters were Thanksgivings at Aunt Pat's house in Henderson. The three bedroom house brimmed over with family and the food was bountiful and magnificent! Among the spread was always Aunt Pat's praline sweet potatoes.

The most amazing part of this sweet delight was that they attracted me, a child who despised pecans! The richness of the butter and sweet potatoes combined with the sweet crunchy, almost toffee- like, topping of roasted pecans drew me to the dish, pecan detestation or no. The paradoxical dichotomy of its savory sweetness rested in my mind for the year as my palette patiently waited for its return the next Thanksgiving. The dish itself was the embodiment of autumn!

As the sisters' families continued to grow, each sister began having her own Thanksgiving with her immediate family. I was greatly disappointed to not have Thanksgiving with my Great Aunts and cousins any longer, but the absence of Aunt Pat's praline sweet potatoes was the most devastating loss to a young lady who adores food as much as I do. So imagine my joy at the sight of my Grammie walking through my mother's back door, carrying her Thanksgiving Day contribution which included Aunt Pat's praline sweet potatoes!

Pat's Brown Sugar Pound Cake

1 c. shortening
½ c. butter, softened
(1) 1-lb. box light brown sugar
5 large eggs
3 c. all-purpose flour
½ tsp. of salt
½ tsp. baking powder
1 c. evaporated milk
1 tsp. maple flavoring or vanilla extract
Brown Sugar Glaze

Beat the shortening, butter and brown sugar at medium speed with an electric mixer 2 minutes or until creamy. Add eggs, 1 at a time, beating well after each addition. Combine flour, salt, and baking powder; add alternately with milk, beginning and ending with flour mixture. Stir in flavoring Pour batter into a greased and floured 12 c. bundt pan.

Bake at 300 degrees for 1 hour and 15 minutes or until a long wooden pick inserted in the center comes out clean. Cool in pan on a wire rack 15 minutes; remove from pan, and cool completely on a wire rack. Pour warm *Brown Sugar Glaze over cake. Let cake stand 30 minutes or until glaze is firm.

Brown Sugar Glaze

½ c. butter
1 c. firmly packed light brown sugar
¼ c. evaporated milk
3 c. powdered sugar, sifted
1 tsp. vanilla extract

Melt butter in a medium saucepan over medium heat. Whisk in brown sugar and cook 1 minute. Add milk, powdered sugar, and vanilla; whisk until creamy. Remove from heat and pour immediately over cooled cake.

Pat's Buttermilk Pie

3 and ¾ c. sugar
4 Tbsp.s all-purpose flour
6 eggs
1 c. buttermilk
1 c. butter, melted
2 tsp.s vanilla
2 unbaked pie shells
Preheat oven to 450 degrees. Combine sugar, flour, eggs, buttermilk, butter, and vanilla. Mix until well blended. Pour into pie shells. Bake for 10 minutes. Reduce heat to 350 degrees and bake for about 45 additional minutes or until set.

Pat's Caramel Chocolate Nut Bars

14 oz. pkg Kraft caramels
6 oz. pkg Nestles chocolate chips
2/3 c. Pet Milk
1 ½ sticks margarine (softened to room temperature)
1 pkg. German Choc. Cake mix
1c. chopped nuts
Melt caramels in 1/3 c. milk. Remove from heat. Mix cake mix, 1/3 c. milk and margarine and nuts. This will be stiff. Sprinkle ½ of this in greased pan. Bake at 350 degrees for 6 minutes. Remove from oven. Sprinkle chocolate chips on top. Pour caramel mixture on top. Sprinkle remaining cake mixture on top. Bake 15 minutes at 350 degrees. Cool well before cutting.

Pat's Cream Cheese Bars

1 box yellow cake mix
2 eggs
1 stick margarine
Mix by hand and pat into greased
and floured 9x13 pan.
Mix together:
1 box powdered sugar
8 oz. pkg. Cream cheese
2 eggs
Coconut or nuts (optional)
Pour on first mixture and bake 45
minutes at 350 degrees.

Pat's Praline Sweet Potatoes

3 c. mashed sweet potatoes
1 c. sugar
2 eggs
1 tsp. vanilla
½ c. melted margarine

Mix and pour in 2 qt. casserole and
top with:
1 c. brown sugar
1/3 c. soft margarine
1 c. chopped nuts
Bake 50 minutes at 350 degrees.

Patsy and Tommie

Pat's Festive Cranberry Salad

1 can (20 oz.) crushed pineapple, undrained
2 pkg. (4- serving size each)
OR 1 pkg. (8- serving size)
raspberry gelatin
1 can (16 oz.) whole cranberry
sauce
1 medium apple, chopped
2/3 c. chopped walnuts

Drain pineapple,
reserving liquid in a 1-quart
liquid measuring c.. Remove
1 Tbsp. of the crushed pineapple; set aside for garnish.
Add enough cold water to the
reserved liquid to measure 3
c.; Pour into large saucepan.
Bring to a boil; remove from
heat. Add gelatin; stir at least
2 minutes until completely
dissolved. Add cranberry
sauce; stir together (gelatin
mixture should be thick). Pour
into large bowl.

Refrigerate for 1 ½ hours
or until slightly thickened
(consistency of unbeaten egg
whites). Stir in remaining
pineapple, apples, and walnuts;
stir gently. Pour into medium
serving bowl. Refrigerate 4
hours or until firm. Top with
reserved crushed pineapple
just before serving

Patsy, Sandy (Frances's cocker
spaniel), and Tommie

Pat's Cream Cheese Pound Cake

3 sticks unsalted butter
8 oz. Cream cheese
3 c. sugar
3 c. cake flour
6 eggs
Pinch of salt
1 Tbsp. vanilla

Cream butter and cream cheese,
and add sugar. Beat until light and
fluffy. Alternately add 1 c. of flour
with 2 eggs and salt until all eggs
and flour have been added. Mix
very well. Add vanilla, and pour
into tube pan, which has been
greased and floured or sprayed
well. Put in cold oven, set at 300
degrees (turn it on), and bake at
this temperature for 1 hour. Raise
temperature to 350 degrees and
bake for an additional 15 minutes.

Patsy's Pumpkin Bread

½ tsp. nutmeg
1 tsp. cinnamon
3 c. sugar
1 c. of corn oil (vegetable or canola)
4 eggs
½ tsp. of salt
1 c. canned pumpkin
1 c. water
2 tsp.s soda
3 c. flour
Nuts (as desired)

Beat first six ingredients together. Blend remaining ingredients in order listed. Grease three 1 lb. coffee cans. Fill each ½ full. Bake 1 hour at 350 degrees. Let cool for 10 minutes before removing from cans. Store in refrigerator or freezer.

Pat's Yam Pie

2 c. cooked sweet potatoes
2 c. sugar
½ c. cream
1 stick butter
1 egg
½ tsp. vanilla

Cook potatoes, mash. Mix with other ingredients. Pour into unbaked pie crust. Bake in 350 degree oven for about 50 minutes or until done.

Patsy and Tommie Picture on the middle right: Patsy's skirt was handmade by herself and Tommie's skirt was made by her Grandmother Melton, out of bandanas

June and Patsy, 2003

Christmastime at Patsy's

Back, left to right: June, Kathryn, Sandy, Betty, and Patsy
Front, left to right: Drorothy, Tommie, and Frances

Tommie Jean
Melton Akin

Grammie's Caramel Pies
20"x35"
Acrylic paint, gold leaf, grave rubbing, and faux pearls on wooden panel

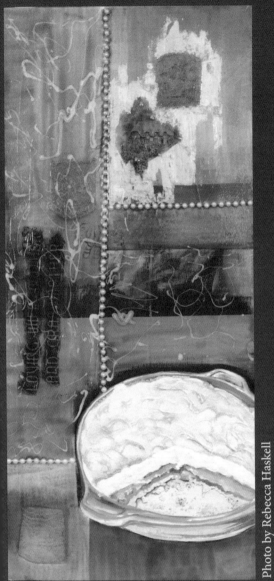

Photo by Rebecca Haskell

Born: December 4, 1935
Married: Harold Rayford Akin
Children: Janice Akin Pleasant, Lisa Akin Ryan, and Stacy Melton Akin

I have never heard of caramel pies from anyone other than my Grammie, Tommie Jean Melton Akin. So it stands to reason that to me, she makes the best caramel pies ever! Being Big Mama's baby girl, my Grammie is an excellent cook. But being a Melton girl, her expert sweet tooth makes her an even better baker.

My earliest memories of her baking skills include two main sweet staples: coconut cake and caramel pie. Now I had experienced coconut cake as a child, but never had I experienced caramel pie, nor have I experienced it anywhere or by anyone other than my Grammie, since my childhood.

As I understand it, Grammie acquired her caramel pie recipe from her mother-in-law, my Poppy's mother, Mary Elizabeth Sledge Akin, affectionately known as "Mamaw." Mamaw regularly prepared caramel pies for Sunday afternoon deserts; however, she died when I was just an infant, so I never experienced her caramel legacy, except through Grammie, who has carried the caramel pie recipe into infamy. It is a favorite among all the men in my immediate family (including my own father who has been divorced from my mother since I was four… he still requests a caramel pie on a regular basis).

I am thankful that I have never known another caramel pie pastry practitioner. My Grammie doesn't share a spotlight with anyone when it comes to this delectable desert. It is her heart winning recipe. She is the sole creator of a sugar legend. I am so proud to own the recipe and share it with others, but I am most proud that I am the granddaughter of a sweet-specialist.

Tommie's Caramel Pie
(Jan's handwriting)

Recipe for *Caramel Pie* Serves *8*
from the kitchen of *Mary E. Akin Via Jan*
Pleasant

½ c. sugar divided 1c + ½ c.
3 Tbs. flour
3 eggs
¼ c. butter - real butter plus water to make 2 c.
1 C. evaporated milk 3 1 tsp. vanilla
1 unbaked pie shell - baked if preferred

Combine flour + ½ c sugar, separate egg yolks + whites, set whites aside for meringue. Add egg yolks to sugar mixture and beat till well mixed, set aside. In cast iron skillet, heat 1 C. sugar over mod heat stirring constantly until sugar browns to a golden dark brown color, but will burn easily. When color reached, add egg + milk mixture, stirring constantly (*Don't worry it's not ruined!*) keep stirring till all becomes creamy. Add ¼ c. butter + 1 tsp vanilla. Put in shell + bake 375° till shell browns. Top w/ Meringue + bake 350° Till meringue sets + light brown.

Tommie (left) and the Minden Cheerleaders

Tommie's Baked Bean Broil

(made it while kids were growing up)
1 can pork and beans
2 Tbsp.s pickle relish
½ tsp. prepared mustard
4 hamburger buns, split
16 thin strips cheddar cheese
8 slices of bacon, cut in half and partially cooked

Combine beans, relish, and mustard. Spoon onto the bun halves. Top each with strips of cheese and bacon. Place on cookie sheet and broil until bacon is done and beans are hot (about 3 minutes).

Tommie's Cherry Delight

1 large tub Cool Whip
1 can pineapple chunks
½ c. nuts
1 can sweetened condensed milk Few drops red coloring 1 can cherry pie filling Mix all fruit and condensed milk. Fold in Cool Whip.

Tommie's Chicken fried Steak

Round steak, tenderized. Salt and let it set. Beat an egg and add sweet milk. Dip steak in egg mixture, roll steak in flour, and pan fry in canola oil.

Tommie's Creamed Corn

1 can cream corn, one can whole kernel, ¾ stick of butter

SCHOOL DAYS

Lunn Jarrell, Tommie, and Jo Beth Jarrell

Tommie's Chicken Spaghetti
(her handwriting)

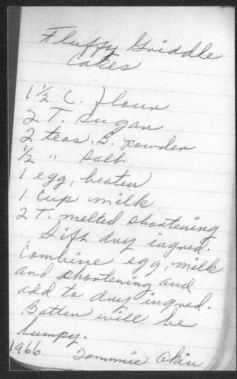

Chicken Spaghetti
1 Hen (boiled)
1 cup of celery (chopped)
1 cup of bell pepper (chopped)
1 cup of chopped onion
1 or 2 quarts of broth
1 can of mushroom soup
1 can of tomato soup
1 lb. of Veletta cheese
salt & pepper - garlic salt
Leave broth in pan & add soups
& veg. Bring to boil til veg
done & stir in cheese & chicken
& simmer a little while.

Tommie's Fluffy Griddle Cakes

Fluffy Griddle
Cakes

1½ c. flour
2 T. Sugar
2 teas. B. Powder
½ " Salt
1 egg, beaten
1 cup milk
2 T. melted shortening
Sift dry ingred.
Combine egg, milk
and shortening and
add to dry ingred.
Batter will be
lumpy.
1966   Tommie Akin

Tommie's Million Dollar Fudge

(3) 4 ½ oz. Plain Hershey bars broken into pieces
(2) 6 oz. pkgs. Chocolate Chips
1 pint Marshmallow Cream
1 Tbsp Butter
1 lb. Pecans
1 tsp Vanilla
4 ½ c. sugar
1 tall can Evaporated milk
Mix Hershey bars, chocolate chips, marshmallow cream, vanilla and butter in a 6 to 8 qt. container. In a 6 qt. Saucepan bring milk and sugar to a boil. After it starts to boil, cook for 6 minutes. Pour sugar mixture over remaining ingredients and stir until smooth and creamy. Fold in pecans. Drop balls of mixture onto wax paper. Let stand 4 to six hours or until completely chilled before removing from wax paper. Makes 6 pounds.

Tommie's Hot Sauce

1 large can tomatoes
2 Tbsp oil
2-3 Tbsp vinegar
2-3 Tbsp crushed red pepper
2-3 cloves crushed garlic
Salt and pepper to taste
Simmer a minute or two. Chill and serve. Better if set over night.

Tommie's Italian Cream Cake
(her handwriting)

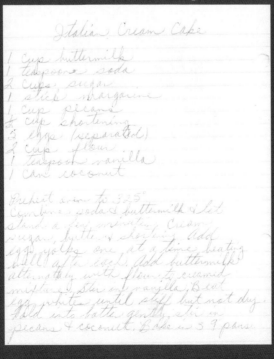

Italian Cream Cake
1 cup buttermilk
1 teaspoon soda
2 cups sugar
1 stick margarine
1 cup pecans
½ cup shortening
5 eggs (separated)
2 cup flour
1 teaspoon vanilla
1 can coconut

Preheat oven to 325°.
Combine soda & buttermilk & let
stand a few minutes. Cream
sugar, butter & shortening. Add
egg yolks one at a time beating
well after each. Add buttermilk
alternately with flour to creamed
mixture. Stir in vanilla. Beat
egg whites until stiff but not dry.
Fold into batter gently. Stir in
pecans & coconut. Bake in 3 9 pans.

Tommie's Millionaires
(her handwriting)

millionaires

2 pkgs. Kraft caramels
⅓ stick Oleo
⅔ c. Angel flake coconut (opt.)
¼ stick paraffin
2 cups coarsely chopped pecans
2 tablespoons water
3 jumbo Hersheys

Melt caramels with 2 tablespoons water in top of a double boiler, add oleo, when melted add pecans (and coconut if desired.) Drop by teaspoons onto waxed paper. Cool (may be cooled in refrigerator.) Melt Hersheys + paraffin in a double boiler. Dip caramels into chocolate + place on buttered wax paper. Do not refrigerate.

Tommie's Oatmeal Cake
(her handwriting)

Oatmeal Cake

Soak a few minutes:
  1 cup oats
  1½ cups hot water

Cream:
  1 cup sugar
  1 cup Brown Sugar
  ½ cup Shortening
  2 Eggs
  1⅓ cup flour
  ½ tsp. salt
  1 tsp. soda
  1 tsp. cinnamon

Icing

1 stick butter
1 cup Brown Sugar
4 Tablespoons pet milk
Boil one minute.
1 cup coconut
1 cup nuts

Tommie's Old Fashioned Fudge
(from Melvin and Juanita Cooper)

1/3 c. milk
2 to 3 Tbsp Cocoa
2 Tbsp butter
1 c. sugar
2 Tbsp corn syrup
2 tsp vanilla
Pinch of salt
Cook all ingredients together until soft ball stage. Beat until it loses gloss and pour into buttered dish.

Tommie's Molasses Cookies

¾ c. shortening
1 c. sugar
¼ c. molasses
1 egg
2 tsp.s baking soda
2 c. sifted all purpose flour
½ tsp. cloves
½ tsp. ginger
1 tsp. cinnamon
½ tsp. salt

Melt shortening in a 4 or 4 quart saucepan over low heat. Remove from heat; allow to cool. Then add sugar, molasses, and egg; beat well. Sift together flour, soda, cloves, ginger, cinnamon, and salt. Add these to the first mixture. Mix well and chill thoroughly. Form one-inch balls; roll in granulated sugar and place on greased cookie sheets two inches apart. Bake at 375 degrees for eight to ten minutes. Makes about four dozen cookies.

Left to Right: Tommie, Pearl (Big Mama), and Sandy. Sandy lived with Big Mama and Big Daddy in Minden while Dorothy and Millard moved around with Millard's military career. She was often referrred to as "the 8th sister."

Harold Rayford Akin and Tommie Melton (Akin)

Tommie's Peanut Pattie

3 c. sugar
1 c. water
1 c. light corn syrup
1 lb. Peanuts (raw)
6 drops red food coloring
½ c. salted butter

Bring sugar, water, and syrup to boil. Add peanuts and coloring. Cook over medium heat until hard ball stage. Remove from flame. Add butter and salt. Beat until thickened and loses its gloss. Pour onto greased cookie sheet. Break into pieces when cooled.

Tommie's Pot Roast Meat Loaf
 (made it while kids were growing up)

1 lb. lean ground beef
2/3 c. evaporated milk
1/3 c. fine dry bread crumbs
¼ c. ketchup or chili sauce
1 tsp. salt
2 tsp.s Worcestershire sauce
¼ tsp. pepper

Mix all the above ingredients and shape into a loaf in the center of a 13x9x2- inch pan.

Peel and slice ¼ inch thick 3 medium potatoes and 3 medium onions. Peel and quarter lengthwise 3 medium carrots. Mix together 2 tsp.s of dried parsley flakes, 1 tsp. of salt, and a dash of pepper. Place vegetables in layers around meat. Sprinkle each layer with part of the salt mixture. Cover tightly with foil. Bake at 375 degrees for 1 hour or until vegetables are tender. Uncover and bake 10 minutes more to brown meat. Serves 4.

Tommie's Plain Cake (Pound Cake, from Mary Elizabeth Akin)

2 sticks of butter
1 ½ c sugar
5 eggs
2 c. flour
2 tsp lemon flavoring
Cream butter and sugar. Add eggs gradually. Mix in flour gradually. Add lemon flavoring. Bake 1 hour at 350 degrees until golden.

Tommie's Pink Cranberry Freeze

(1) 8 oz. package cream cheese
2 Tbsp.s sugar
2 Tbsp.s mayonnaise

Beat the above ingredients with a mixer, and stir in by hand the following:
(1) 8 oz. can crushed pineapple, with juice
1 can whole cranberry sauce
½ c. chopped pecans
(1) 8 oz. container frozen whipped topping

Mix gently and pour into a 7x11 inch pan or in individual muffin c. or molds. Freeze until very firm. Makes about 20 servings.

Tommie's Peanut Butter Fudge

5 c. sugar
1 large can Pet milk
Cook to soft ball stage. Remove from heat and add 1 tsp. of vanilla and one 12 oz. Jar peanut butter.

Tommie's Special K Cookies

1 c. light Karo
1 c. sugar
1 tsp vanilla
4 c. Special K or Cocoa Puffs
(per Tommie)
1 ½ c. crunchy peanut butter
1 c. coconut
Mix together in saucepan
Karo, sugar, and vanilla and
boil until it bubbles. Remove
from heat and mix in cereal,
peanut butter, and coconut.
Drop by spoonfuls onto wax
paper to cool.

Tommie's Teacakes/ Sugar Cookies

3 eggs
2 c. Sugar
1 c. Buttermilk
1 c. Crisco shortening
3 tsp baking powder
2 Tbsp vanilla
3 c. Flour
Cream shortening and sugar. Beat in eggs. Add in buttermilk and
vanilla. Mix baking powder and soda into the flour and add to
mixture. Roll out onto floured board. Cut out with cookie cutter.
Bake at 375 for 10 minutes.

Tommie's To Die for Pot Roast
(made it while kids were growing up)

1 Pot Roast, about 3 lbs.
1 pkg. Ranch dressing dry mix, about 0.4 oz.
1 pkg. Italian dressing mix, about 0.6 oz.
1 pkg. brown gravy mix, about 1.6 oz
½ c. warm water
Mix contents of all three packages with water and pour over roast that has
been placed in the crock pot. Cook on low for 6-7 hours. You can add another
½ c. water if you want more gravy.

Tommie's Spoon Burgers
(Auntie's handwriting)

Tommie's Spoon
Burgers

1 lb. Ground Chuck
1 Can Chicken
Gumbo soup
½ soup can
water
1 onion Chopped
1 T. Catsup
1 T. salad
mustard
Brown meat
and onion. add
other ingredients
and cook down
low. Serve on
toasted buns.

Tommie's Texas Pecan Cake
(her handwriting)

Texas Pecan Cake
5 c flour
3 c sugar
7 eggs, beat yolks + white
separately
2 oz. lemon extract
1 tsp. soda
4 tbls. wine (room temp)
1 lb. pecans (cut up)
½ lb. red candied cherries (chopped)
½ lb. green " "
½ box white raisins
½ box black "
1 lb. margarine or butter
1 lb. glazed pineapple (cut up)
Cream butter + sugar – add
other ingredients. Fold in
stiffly beaten egg whites last

Bake in tube pan, lightly
greased + lined with wax
paper. Use foil over + under
cake pan 4 hrs. at 250°.

Recipe from Tommy

"My mother, Tommie Akin, grew up as the young-est of seven girls who belonged to Hubert Sample Melton and Pearl Janette Cooper Melton. No doubt as the "baby" she was slightly "spoiled," but I think that is maybe what made her the mother she has been. I remember as a preschooler we played "Go Fish" and "Old Maid" with circus printed playing cards almost daily. She read to us lot. Oh, the little Golden Book collection we had was wonderful. She still has it! There was a never ending supply of fresh home baked cookies because that was her 'thing'. She BAKED! She was and still is good at it. I know those things were modeled to her by her older sisters and her mother, my grandmother, affectionately known as Big Mama.

Big Mama was one of the most amazing women I have ever been so blessed to have had in my life. She was so ever-present in our lives her entire time on this earth. She was involved in all seven of her daughters' families. Even though four of those daughters lived a distance away, they always made time to come home. I remember Sunday lunches with as many present as possible. In the "old Minden house days," she made the absolute best fried chicken and homestyle "creamed" potatoes in the world, all served on Blue Willow plates, accom-panied with hot rolls and dozens of dessert choices. She always fed people. even when she and Big Daddy moved into town (Henderson). There was always lunch at her house because someone was there. On any given weekday it could be my cousin Dewayne or myself on lunch hour from work or school. It could be her sister, sister-in-law, or other cousins come to visit.

In the back yard of the Henderson house, she had an apple tree that made a very small tart apple but her pies with those apples were the best! My sister and I spent a year with Big Mama when my Dad took a promotion and my parents had to move before school was out. That was a year I will always remember. She had lots of knowledge to impart to me, which she did! I was 17 and did not realize how valuable it would be one day."

- Jan Akin Pleasant

January 2003 at Jan Akin Pleasant's home.

This picture was the last of all seven sisters together. The following March Aunt Betty passed away from stomach cancer.

Back, left to right: Betty, Patsy, Tommie, and Kathryn
Front, left to right: June, Frances, and Dorothy